everyday

GoodFood
Meals for one

Editor **Cassie Bes**

BOOKS

Contents

GoodFood
Meals for one

10 9 8 7 6 5 4 3 2 1

Published in 2013 by BBC Books, an imprint of Ebury Publishing
A Random House Group company

Photographs © BBC Worldwide 2013
Recipes © BBC Worldwide 2013
Book design © Woodlands Books Ltd 2013
All recipes contained in this book first appeared in BBC *Good Food* magazine.

The Random House Group Limited
Reg. No. 954009

Addresses for companies within the Random House Group can be found at www.randomhouse.co.uk

A CIP catalogue record for this book is available from the British Library

The Random House Group Limited supports the Forest Stewardship Council® (FSC®), the leading international forest-certification organisation. Our books carrying the FSC label are printed on FSC®-certified paper. FSC is the only forest-certification scheme supported by the leading environmental organisations, including Greenpeace. Our paper procurement policy can be found at www.randomhouse.co.uk/environment

To buy books by your favourite authors and register for offers visit www.randomhouse.co.uk

Printed and bound by Firmengruppe APPL, aprinta druck, Wemding, Germany
Colour origination by Dot Gradations Ltd, UK

Commissioning Editor: Muna Reyal
Project Editor: Lizzy Gaisford
Designer: Kathryn Gammon
Production: Alex Goddard
Picture Researcher: Gabby Harrington

ISBN: 9781849906715

Picture credits

BBC *Good Food* magazine and BBC Books would like to thank the following people for providing photos. While every effort has been made to trace and acknowledge all photographers, we should like to apologise should there be any errors or omissions.

Carolyn Barber p87; Peter Cassidy p199; Will Heap p27, p29, p33, p37, p45, p57, p83, p99, p145, p119, p139, p147, p201; Lara Holmes p77, p109, p117, p127, p185; Jonathan Kennedy p15, p17, p53, p65, p155, p159, p175; Adrian Lawrence p25, p75, p59, p151, p165; William Lingwood p209; Gareth Morgans p35, p61, p101, p103, p107, p113, p131, p177; David Munns p11, p21, p49, p51, p55, p63, p73, p89, p95, p97, p111, p135, p157, p163, p167, p173, p179, p195; Myles New p85, p141, p207, p211; Stuart Ovenden p23, p69, p71, p79, p91, p115, p105, p161, p205, p197; Lis Parsons p13, p19, p43, p47, p81, p93, p121, p123, p169, p183, p187, p189, p191, p193; Charlie Richards p171; Howard Shooter p129, p143, p137; Roger Stowell p39, p203; Yuki Sugiura p67; Philip Webb p149, p181; Jon Whitaker p31, p41, p.133, p153

All the recipes in this book were created by the editorial team at *Good Food* and by regular contributors to BBC Magazines.

Introduction

Whether you want a night in with some tasty food, speedy snacks to take in to work or an easy and delicious recipe to save in batches and eat for the week, this book is crammed full of exciting recipes perfect for single servings.

Often when cooking for one you find yourself with leftover food, which just gets wasted, but you can avoid this simply by adjusting your shopping habits. When buying fruit or vegetables, it is tempting to buy multi-packs which seem to be great value, but picking loose, individual items means you buy only what you need. You'll see that many of the recipes in this book specify using '1 small carrot' or '1 small pepper' to avoid waste. Many of the recipes also use shallots in place of onions, as one shallot is often the perfect amount for a single serving. It is also well worth making friends with your local butcher and fishmonger (or visiting the counters in your supermarket) where you can buy individual items.

Inevitably you will find that you need to buy bigger packets for certain recipes, but if so, remember the freezer is your friend! Lots of the recipes in this book can be easily doubled, or even quadrupled, and portions can be frozen for another day. Just remember to defrost thoroughly in the fridge overnight before reheating.

Cooking for one shouldn't be seen as a chore, instead we should embrace it as an opportunity to spoil ourselves and indulge in the things we love. Your husband doesn't like fish? Well, put mackerel on the menu tonight! We all deserve to treat ourselves, so flick through to the 'Special suppers' chapter; all the recipes are simple, but special enough to make eating alone feel like a luxury, instead of a necessity.

Cassie

Cassie Best
Good Food magazine

Notes and conversion tables

NOTES ON THE RECIPES
• Eggs are large in the UK and Australia and extra large in America unless stated otherwise.
• Wash fresh produce before preparation.
• Recipes contain nutritional analyses for 'sugar', which means the total sugar content including all natural sugars in the ingredients, unless otherwise stated.

OVEN TEMPERATURES

Gas	°C	°C Fan	°F	Oven temp.
¼	110	90	225	Very cool
½	120	100	250	Very cool
1	140	120	275	Cool or slow
2	150	130	300	Cool or slow
3	160	140	325	Warm
4	180	160	350	Moderate
5	190	170	375	Moderately hot
6	200	180	400	Fairly hot
7	220	200	425	Hot
8	230	210	450	Very hot
9	240	220	475	Very hot

APPROXIMATE WEIGHT CONVERSIONS
• All the recipes in this book list both imperial and metric measurements. Conversions are approximate and have been rounded up or down. Follow one set of measurements only; do not mix the two.
• Cup measurements, which are used by cooks in Australia and America, have not been listed here as they vary from ingredient to ingredient. Kitchen scales should be used to measure dry/solid ingredients.

Good Food are concerned about sustainable sourcing and animal welfare so where possible we use organic ingredients, humanely reared meats, sustainably caught fish, free-range chickens and eggs and unrefined sugar.

SPOON MEASURES

Spoon measurements are level unless otherwise specified.

• 1 teaspoon (tsp) = 5ml
• 1 tablespoon (tbsp) = 15ml
• 1 Australian tablespoon = 20ml (cooks in Australia should measure 3 teaspoons where 1 tablespoon is specified in a recipe)

APPROXIMATE LIQUID CONVERSIONS

metric	imperial	AUS	US
50ml	2fl oz	¼ cup	¼ cup
125ml	4fl oz	½ cup	½ cup
175ml	6fl oz	¾ cup	¾ cup
225ml	8fl oz	1 cup	1 cup
300ml	10fl oz/½ pint	½ pint	1¼ cups
450ml	16fl oz	2 cups	2 cups/1 pint
600ml	20fl oz/1 pint	1 pint	2½ cups
1 litre	35fl oz/1¾ pints	1¾ pints	1 quart

Super green mackerel salad

Packed with omega-3, vitamin C, iron, calcium, fibre and two of your 5-a-day, this superfood salad is not only incredibly good for you but tastes delicious too.

TAKES 18 MINUTES ● SERVES 1

85g/3oz green beans, trimmed
85g/3oz thin-stemmed broccoli
large handful baby leaf spinach
2 hot-smoked mackerel fillets, skinned
   and flaked
2 tsp sunflower seeds, toasted

FOR THE DRESSING

75g/2½ oz low-fat natural yogurt
1 tsp lemon juice
1 tsp wholegrain mustard
2 tsp dill leaves, chopped, plus extra
   to garnish

1 Boil a pan of water. Add the green beans and cook for 2 minutes, then add the broccoli and cook for 2 minutes more. Drain, run under cold water until cool, then drain again well.
2 To make the dressing, combine all the ingredients in a small jam jar with a twist of black pepper, put the lid on and give it a good shake.
3 To serve, mix together the cooked veg with the spinach and mackerel, and pack into a lunchbox. Just before eating, pour over the dressing, scatter over the sunflower seeds and add a grind of black pepper and the extra dill.

PER SERVING 425 kcals, protein 27g, carbs 12g, fat 30g, sat fat 6g, fibre 6g, sugar 10g, salt 2g

Salt-beef club with Cajun fries

An indulgent solo supper of a layered sandwich with sliced beef, creamy dressing and homemade chips.

TAKES 35 MINUTES ● SERVES 1

1 big potato, cut into thin chips
2 tsp olive oil
½ tsp Cajun seasoning
1 heaped tbsp mayonnaise
1 tsp snipped chives
1 tsp Dijon mustard
3 slices white or brown bread, lightly
    toasted
2 radishes, thinly sliced
1 baby or ½ avocado, sliced
2 slices salt beef
couple Little Gem lettuce leaves

1 Heat oven to 200C/180C fan/gas 6. Put the chips on a non-stick baking sheet, toss with the oil and Cajun seasoning, then spread out in a single layer. Pop in the oven and bake, turning once, for 20–25 minutes or until golden and crisp then season.

2 Meanwhile, mix the mayonnaise, chives and mustard in a small bowl, and season. Spread the mix on to 2 of the toasted bread slices. Layer 1 of the spread slices with radishes and avocado. Put the other slice, spread-side up, on top and add the salt beef and lettuce. Top with the final slice.

3 Cut up and secure with cocktail sticks, if you like, then serve alongside the fries.

PER SERVING 825 kcals, protein 21g, carbs 63g, fat 54g, sat fat 10g, fibre 8g, sugar 6g, salt 2.6g

Sweet jacket potato with piri-piri prawns

Swap your baked spud for the sweeter version which are packed with nutrients and taste delicious with these spicy pepper prawns.

TAKES 55 MINUTES ● SERVES 1

1 large sweet potato
2½ tsp olive oil
1 garlic clove, crushed
1 small red pointed pepper, deseeded
    and sliced into rings
pinch chilli flakes
½ tsp sweet paprika
1 tbsp red wine vinegar
1 tbsp tomato ketchup
100g/4oz raw peeled king prawns
few sprigs parsley, chopped
2 tbsp light mayonnaise

1 Heat oven to 200C/180C fan/gas 6. Put the sweet potato on a baking sheet, rub all over with a little of the oil and season with some salt. Bake for 45 minutes until really soft.

2 Meanwhile, heat the remaining oil in a frying pan. Add the garlic and pepper, and cook for 2 minutes, making sure the garlic doesn't burn. Add the chilli flakes, half the paprika, the vinegar, ketchup, 1 tablespoon water and the prawns to the pan, then bubble for 2 minutes until the prawns are cooked through. Stir through most of the parsley, saving a little to sprinkle over at the end.

3 Mix the remaining paprika into the mayonnaise. Once the potato is cooked, split it down the centre, pile in the prawn mixture and dollop the paprika mayo on top. Scatter over the remaining parsley and serve.

PER SERVING 425 kcals, protein 22g, carbs 46g, fat 17g, sat fat 3g, fibre 9g, sugar 22g, salt 1.9g

Moroccan turkey salad

Use up leftover roast meat in this healthy Moroccan-inspired salad.

TAKES 35 MINUTES ● SERVES 1

2 tsp olive oil
1 small pitta bread
½ small aubergine, diced
1½ tsp harissa paste
75g/2½oz cherry tomatoes, halved
140g/5oz cooked chicken or turkey
    breast, shredded
handful rocket leaves
2 tbsp pomegranate seeds
a few mint leaves, to garnish

1 Heat the olive oil in a pan, tear the pitta into pieces and fry in the oil until crisp. Tip into a bowl.

2 Fry the aubergine in the same pan for 10–15 minutes until soft. Add to the pitta with the harissa, tomatoes, chicken or turkey and rocket. Toss well. Scatter over the pomegranate seeds and mint leaves, and serve.

PER SERVING 360 kcals, protein 47g, carbs 22g, fat 9g, sat fat 2g, fibre 4g, sugar 6g, salt 0.6g

Cranberry & Stilton toastie

Cheddar, Brie or goat's cheese would all work well as an alternative to Stilton in this tasty toasted sandwich – use whatever cheese you have to hand!

TAKES 15 MINUTES ● MAKES 1
large knob softened butter
2 slices white bloomer bread
50g/2oz crumbled Stilton
1 spring onion, sliced
1–2 tbsp cranberry jelly

1 Butter both slices of the bloomer. Make into a sandwich with the Stilton, spring onion and cranberry jelly, keeping the butter on the outside of the bread. Fry in a non-stick griddle or frying pan for 3–4 minutes on each side. Keep the heat gentle so the cheese melts slowly as the bread becomes golden and crunchy. Serve warm.

PER TOASTIE 604 kcals, protein 19g, carbs 45g, fat 40g, sat fat 24g, fibre 2g, sugar 9g, salt 2.5g

Hot-smoked salmon with fennel salad & lemon mayo

This tasty salad will stay crisp and fresh if packed into a lunchbox; just store the mayo separately in a tub and stir through before serving.

TAKES 10 MINUTES • SERVES 1

squeeze lemon juice
3 tbsp light mayonnaise
few sprigs dill, chopped
½ fennel bulb, cored and thinly sliced
¼ cucumber, peeled lengthways into
   ribbons
1 tbsp white wine vinegar
2 tsp olive oil
handful watercress leaves
1 hot-smoked peppered salmon fillet

1 Mix together the lemon juice, mayonnaise, a little of the dill and some seasoning, then spoon into a ramekin or a tub. Set aside.

2 In a large bowl, mix together the remaining dill, fennel and cucumber, season, then drizzle over the vinegar and oil.

3 Put the watercress on to a plate, or into a plastic container to take to work, and top with the fennel salad. Flake the salmon on the side and serve with the lemon mayo.

PER SERVING 534 kcals, protein 28g, carbs 11g, fat 42g, sat fat 6g, fibre 6g, sugar 8g, salt 3.8g

Griddled pear & blue cheese salad

Sweet pear and salty blue cheese is a classic combination – add a handful of toasted walnuts for a little crunch, if you like.

TAKES 20 MINUTES ● SERVES 1

1 firm ripe pear, sliced lengthways into
   1cm/½in slices
1½ tsp olive oil
½ tbsp white wine vinegar
1 tsp clear honey
handful mixed salad leaves
50g/2oz blue cheese, crumbled
crusty bread, to serve (optional)

1 Put the sliced pear in a bowl and drizzle with ½ teaspoon of the oil. Heat a griddle pan, then cook the pear for 1 minute on each side. Set aside to cool.
2 Mix the remaining oil, the vinegar and the honey to make a dressing. Toss together the pear, salad leaves and cheese and drizzle with the dressing. Serve with bread, if you like.

PER SERVING 343 kcals, protein 13g, carbs 20g, fat 23g, sat fat 12g, fibre 5g, sugar 20g, salt 1g

Tartines with roasted tomato & mint pesto

Cheese and tomato sandwiches get a makeover with creamy ricotta, sweet roasted tomatoes and a punchy mint-and-garlic pesto piled on top of toasted bread.

TAKES 30 MINUTES ● SERVES 1

2–3 medium-sized vine-ripened
   tomatoes, halved
1 tbsp extra-virgin olive oil
2–3 thick slices wholemeal bread
½ garlic clove
1 tbsp pine nuts, toasted
small handful mint leaves
splash balsamic vinegar
50g/2oz ricotta
green salad, to serve (optional)

1 Heat oven to 190C/170C fan/gas 5. Put the tomato halves in a roasting tin in a single layer. Drizzle with a little of the oil, season well and roast for 20 minutes. Set aside.

2 Toast the bread, then rub with the garlic (keep the garlic for the pesto). Brush a bit more oil over the bread and put it on to a plate.

3 Using the small bowl of a food processor, or a pestle and mortar, blend together the pine nuts, mint, reserved garlic, remaining oil and balsamic vinegar. Thickly spread the ricotta on the bread, then top with the roasted tomatoes and some mint pesto. Serve with a salad, if you like.

PER TARTINE 442 kcals, protein 14g, carbs 31g, fat 29g, sat fat 6g, fibre 7g, sugar 9g, salt 0.9g

Spiced parsnip & cauliflower soup

This warming soup is superhealthy and easily doubled, so why not double or quadruple the ingredients and freeze the leftovers for another day?

TAKES 50 MINUTES • SERVES 1

1 tsp olive oil
100g/4oz cauliflower, cut into florets
2 parsnips, chopped
1 shallot, chopped
½ tsp fennel seeds
¼ tsp coriander seeds
¼ tsp turmeric powder
1 small garlic clove, sliced
½ green chilli, deseeded and chopped
250ml/9fl oz vegetable stock
small handful coriander leaves, chopped
a grinding of black pepper, to serve (optional)
crusty bread, to serve (optional)

1 Heat the oil in a large pan and add the vegetables. Cover partially with a lid and sweat gently for 10–15 minutes until soft but not brown. In a separate pan, dry-roast the spices with a pinch of salt for a few minutes until fragrant. Grind with a pestle and mortar to a fine powder.

2 Add the garlic, chilli and spices to the vegetables, and cook for about 5 minutes, stirring regularly. Pour in the stock, topping up if necessary just to cover the veg. Simmer for 25–30 minutes, covered with a lid, until all the vegetables are tender.

3 Purée the spicy vegetables with a blender until smooth. Dilute the consistency with more water if needed, until you get a thick but easily pourable soup. Season generously and stir in the coriander. Serve with a grinding of black pepper and crusty bread, if you like.

PER SERVING 280 kcals, protein 11g, carbs 42g, fat 8g, sat fat 1g, fibre 17g, sugar 22g, salt 1.7g

Cottage cheese & pepper sandwich spread

Store this healthy sandwich filling in a container until lunchtime and spread the bread when you're ready to eat to avoid having soggy sandwiches!

TAKES 10 MINUTES • SERVES 1

140g/5oz cottage cheese

½ red pepper, deseeded and thinly sliced

few basil leaves, torn

2 slices sourdough bread or wholemeal bread

drizzle balsamic vinegar

1 Layer the cottage cheese, red pepper and basil with some seasoning in a bowl or plastic container. Chill until lunchtime.

2 Toast the bread and cool for 1 minute, then give the cottage cheese mixture a quick mix and spoon on to the bread. Drizzle with balsamic vinegar, sandwich the bread slices together and eat straight away.

PER SERVING 316 kcals, protein 23g, carbs 40g, fat 7g, sat fat 3g, fibre 2g, sugar 8g, salt 1.8g

Broad bean & feta cheese toasts

This lovely light supper makes for the perfect dinner in the garden. Remove the tough outer skin from the broad beans to enjoy fully the soft, sweet beans inside.

TAKES 30 MINUTES • SERVES 1

175g/6oz broad beans, fresh or frozen
50g/2oz feta, drained
1 tbsp chopped mint leaves
2 tsp extra-virgin olive oil
handful mixed salad leaves
handful cherry tomatoes, halved
1 tsp lemon juice
2 thin slices baguette

1 Bring a small pan of water to the boil. Add the beans, return to the boil and cook for 4 minutes. Drain in a colander under running water until cold. Press each bean out of its skin into a bowl.

2 Crumble the feta over the beans and scatter with the chopped mint. Season with a good grind of black pepper and drizzle with 1 teaspoon of the oil. Toss together.

3 In a separate bowl toss the salad leaves and tomatoes with the remaining olive oil and the lemon juice.

4 Toast the bread under the grill or in a toaster until golden and crisp on both sides. To serve, spoon the bean-and-cheese mixture on to the warm toasts and serve with the salad.

PER SERVING 354 kcals, protein 20g, carbs 28g, fat 18g, sat fat 8g, fibre 11g, sugar 6g, salt 2.2g

Three cheese & onion jacket potato

Swap your usual baked bean filling for something a little more interesting. Let the cheesy filling melt into the potato for a few minutes before serving.

TAKES 1 HOUR • SERVES 1

1 large baking potato
drizzle sunflower or vegetable oil
50g/2oz soft cheese
25g/1oz mozzarella, grated
25g/1oz mature Cheddar, grated
1 tbsp milk
1 spring onion, finely sliced
dollop onion chutney

1 Heat oven to 180C/160C fan/gas 4. Pierce the potato a few times with a sharp knife. Put the potato in the microwave and heat on full for 5 minutes. Transfer to a baking sheet, rub a little oil and a sprinkle of salt all over the skin, then bake in the oven for 45 minutes – 1 hour, until the skin is crisp and the middle is soft.

2 Meanwhile, mix the cheeses, milk and a grind of black pepper in a small bowl. Split the potato in half. Spoon in the cheesy filling, sprinkle over the spring onion and top with the onion chutney.

PER SERVING 662 kcals, protein 20g, carbs 59g, fat 38g, sat fat 24g, fibre 7g, sugar 7g, salt 1.3g

Open chicken-Caesar salad sandwich

Turn this light bite into a hearty salad by chopping the bread into croutons and adding a few cherry tomatoes and salty anchovies.

TAKES 20 MINUTES • MAKES 1

1 boneless skinless chicken breast

drizzle sunflower oil

1 Little Gem lettuce

1 thick slice bread

½ small garlic clove

FOR THE DRESSING

1 tbsp low-fat crème fraîche or Greek yogurt

½ tbsp grated Parmesan, plus a few shavings to garnish

squeeze lemon juice

½ tsp capers, roughly chopped

1 Heat a griddle pan. Rub the chicken with the oil, season with some salt and pepper, then griddle for 7 minutes each side or until cooked through. Set aside to rest. Meanwhile, separate the lettuce leaves.

2 Make the dressing. Mix the crème fraîche or yogurt, Parmesan, lemon juice and capers with ½ tablespoon cold water, then season to taste.

3 Toast the bread and rub with the garlic, then crush the garlic clove and add to the dressing. Slice the warm chicken breasts on the diagonal, then top the toast with lettuce leaves, sliced chicken and a drizzle of the Caesar dressing. Finish with a few shavings of Parmesan.

PER SANDWICH 319 kcals, protein 40g, carbs 24g, fat 8g, sat fat 3g, fibre 2g, sugar 3g, salt 1.01g

Open mackerel sandwich with fennel slaw

This Scandinavian-style sandwich uses rye bread for a sturdy base, but you can swap this for wholemeal or granary if you prefer.

TAKES 15 MINUTES • SERVES 1

1-2 slices rye bread
2 tbsp cream cheese
1 hot-smoked peppered mackerel
  fillets, skinned and flaked
½ fennel bulb, cored and thinly sliced
½ small red onion, thinly sliced
1 tsp small capers
1 lemon, ½ juiced, ½ cut into wedges
1 tbsp extra-virgin olive oil
small bunch chives, snipped

1 Toast the bread until crisp, then spread over the soft cheese. Divide the smoked mackerel between the toasts.
2 In a small bowl, mix together the fennel, onion, capers, lemon juice, oil, chives and some seasoning. Spoon this over the fish toasts and serve with lemon wedges for squeezing over.

PER SERVING 548 kcals, protein 20g, carbs 16g, fat 44g, sat fat 13g, fibre 6g, sugar 5g, salt 2.2g

Roasted onion soup with goat's cheese toast

The cheesy toast takes this soup from a light lunch to something much more substantial. Double the soup ingredients and freeze the leftovers, if you like.

TAKES 1 HOUR 20 MINUTES
● **SERVES 1**
2 large onions, sliced
1 tbsp olive oil
250ml/7fl oz vegetable stock
2 tsp wholegrain mustard
½ tsp Marmite
small handful parsley leaves, roughly chopped, plus extra sprig to garnish
2 thick slices bread
25g/1oz soft goat's cheese, cubed

1 Heat oven to 200C/180C fan/gas 6. Put the onions in a roasting tin with the oil and season with some salt and pepper. Give it a good stir, then roast for 45 minutes, stirring halfway through, until the onions are tinged brown, but not burnt.

2 Tip the onions into a large pan with the stock, mustard and Marmite. Bring to the boil and simmer for 15 minutes, then stir in the parsley. Toast 1 slice of bread then spread over the cheese. Ladle the soup into a bowl, pop the cheesy toast on top and a sprig of parsley. Serve with the extra slice of bread on the side.

PER SERVING 454 kcals, protein 15g, carbs 62g, fat 18g, sat fat 5g, fibre 6g, sugar 16g, salt 2.33g

Healthy salad Niçoise

This French-bistro classic becomes healthier with extra veg and a low-fat dressing drizzled over.

TAKES 20 MINUTES ● SERVES 1

100g/4oz new potatoes, thickly sliced
1 medium egg
50g/2oz green beans, trimmed
1 small romaine lettuce heart, leaves
    separated and washed
4 cherry tomatoes, halved
3 anchovies in olive oil, drained well
100g/4oz tuna steak in spring water,
    drained
1 tbsp reduced-fat mayonnaise

1 Bring a large pan of water to the boil. Add the potatoes and the egg, and cook for 7 minutes. Scoop the egg out of the pan, tip in the green beans and cook for a further 4 minutes. Drain the potatoes, beans and egg in a colander under cold running water until cool. Leave to dry.

2 Peel the egg and cut into quarters. Arrange the lettuce leaves in a shallow bowl. Scatter over the beans, potatoes, tomatoes and egg quarters. Pat the anchovies with kitchen paper to absorb the excess oil and put on top.

3 Flake the tuna into chunks and scatter over the salad. Mix the mayonnaise and 1 tablespoon cold water in a bowl until smooth. Drizzle over the salad and serve.

PER SERVING 351 kcals, protein 27g, carbs 22g, fat 17g, sat fat 4g, fibre 4g, sugar 6g, salt 2.1g

Thai-style chicken & sweet potato parcels

Look out for blocks of creamed coconut in the foreign food aisles of the supermarket or in Asian food stores. If you can't find it, use coconut milk and leave out the water.

TAKES 40 MINUTES • SERVES 1

25g/1oz creamed coconut (from a block)

2 tsp soft brown sugar

1 tsp fish sauce

2 tsp Thai green curry paste

½ sweet potato, peeled and cut into small cubes

1 small red pepper, deseeded and cut into small cubes

1 skinless chicken breast

handful coriander leaves and a few lime wedges, to serve

1 Heat oven to 200C/180C fan/gas 6. Dissolve the creamed coconut with 3 tablespoons boiling water and mix to a smooth paste. Stir in the sugar, fish sauce and curry paste.

2 Place a large piece of baking parchment on a baking sheet. Arrange the sweet potato and pepper in the middle of the paper, clearing a space in the centre. Lay the chicken breast in the space and pour over the sauce. Fold over the top edges of the parchment to form a seal and scrunch up the ends like a sweet wrapper.

3 Cook in the oven for 25–30 minutes or until the chicken is cooked through and the vegetables are tender. Sit the parcel on a dinner plate or shallow bowl and carefully open. Sprinkle with coriander and squeeze over some lime juice, to taste.

PER SERVING 429 kcals, protein 34g, carbs 29g, fat 20g, sat fat 15g, fibre 3g, sugar 18g, salt 1.4g

Stir-fry chilli beef wrap

Buy a thin slice of frying steak from the butcher's counter for this recipe, it will cost you half the price of buying a large pack and will cook in minutes.

TAKES 15 MINUTES, PLUS OPTIONAL MARINATING • SERVES 1

75g/2½oz thin-cut frying steak, very thinly sliced
½ tsp mild chilli powder
good pinch ground cumin
1 garlic clove, finely chopped
1 tsp sunflower oil
½ yellow pepper, deseeded and sliced
½ red onion, thinly sliced
1 tomato, chopped
½ x 400g can black beans, drained
handful fresh coriander
2 soft tortilla wraps

1 Put the steak in a bowl with the spices and garlic and stir well. If you have time, leave to marinate for a couple of hours. Heat the oil in a wok, then tip in the beef and fry for just 1–2 minutes, until it changes colour but is still on the rare side. Remove the beef to a plate.

2 Add the pepper and half the onion and stir-fry in the juices – add a splash of water to get things going and stop it burning. Stir in the tomato and beans, and heat through with plenty of seasoning. Stir in most of the coriander.

3 Meanwhile, heat the tortillas. The best way is directly on the gas flame, as it gives them a lovely charred flavour. Stir the beef into the beans and heat briefly. Serve with the tortillas and the reserved onion and coriander.

PER SERVING 642 kcals, protein 33g, carbs 102g, fat 12g, sat fat 3g, fibre 14g, sugar 11g, salt 1.1g

Lamb & potato kebabs with minty broad beans

If you can, leave the lamb, peppers and potatoes to marinate for 1 hour in the garlic, oil and lemon juice. This will tenderise the meat and soak up all the lovely flavours.

TAKES 30 MINUTES • SERVES 1

50g/2oz baby new potatoes
85g/3oz lean lamb neck, cut into 2.5cm/1in dice
½ red pepper, deseeded and cut into large chunks
1 garlic clove, crushed
drizzle olive oil
juice ½ lemon, plus few wedges to serve
140g/5oz fresh or frozen broad beans
1 tbsp mint sauce

1 Bring a pan of water to the boil, tip in the potatoes and cook for 8–10 minutes until tender. Scoop out the potatoes using a slotted spoon, keeping the cooking water on a gentle boil. Put the lamb, potatoes and pepper in a bowl. Add the garlic, oil and lemon juice. Season, then toss well to coat.

2 Heat a griddle pan over a medium-high heat. Thread the lamb, pepper and potatoes onto 2 pre-soaked wooden kebab skewers. When the pan is hot, grill the kebabs for 3–4 minutes on each side until nicely charred around the edges.

3 Add the broad beans to the boiling water and cook for 5 minutes. Drain and pop the beans out of their skins if you have time. Mix with the mint sauce.

4 Serve the kebabs on top of the beans with lemon wedges for squeezing over.

PER SERVING 329 kcals, protein 26g, carbs 28g, fat 13g, sat fat 5g, fibre 10g, sugar 6g, salt 0.2g

Spiced beef, aubergine & shitake stir-fry

Try something new with mince with this spicy, low-cost stir-fry. The flavoursome sauce would also work well with pork or turkey mince.

TAKES 40 MINUTES ● SERVES 1

2 tsp vegetable oil
100g/4oz extra-lean beef mince
½ small aubergine, sliced and cut into thick strips
¼ red chilli, thinly sliced
1 garlic clove, finely chopped
good handful shiitake mushrooms, sliced
1 spring onion, halved horizontally and sliced lengthways
1 tbsp oyster sauce
1 tsp brown sugar
basmati rice, to serve

1 Heat a drop of the oil in a non-stick wok or large frying pan. Cook the mince, breaking it up with a wooden spoon, for about 10 minutes, or until cooked through. Remove with a slotted spoon and set aside.

2 Heat the remaining oil in the pan and fry the aubergine for about 10 minutes, until tender and cooked through. Add half the chilli, the garlic and mushrooms, then cook for a further few minutes. Return the mince to the pan and add most of the spring onion, the oyster sauce, sugar and 50ml/2fl oz water. Bubble for a few minutes, then serve immediately with boiled rice and the remaining chilli and spring onions scattered on top.

PER SERVING 342 kcals, protein 31g, carbs 13g, fat 18g, sat fat 6g, fibre 4g, sugar 8g, salt 2.2g

Fennel-crusted pork chop with celeriac slaw

The anise flavour of the fennel seeds work perfectly with the earthy celeriac slaw in this dish. You could also try adding half a grated apple for an extra sweet crunch.

TAKES 55 MINUTES ● SERVES 1

1 tsp olive oil
good pinch each fennel seeds and
    dried oregano
pinch chilli flakes
1 pork shoulder chop

FOR THE SLAW

2 tbsp light mayonnaise
1 tsp white wine vinegar
1 tsp Worcestershire sauce
1 tsp wholegrain mustard
pinch sugar
small chunk celeriac, about 50g/2oz,
    cut into matchsticks or shredded
1 small carrot, cut into matchsticks
    or shredded
¼ small red onion, diced

1 Heat oven to 190C/170C fan/gas 5. Put the oil, fennel seeds, oregano, chilli and some seasoning on a shallow plate. Rub the pork chop on both sides in the mixture. Place on a baking tray and roast for 40 minutes.

2 Meanwhile, make the slaw. Put the mayonnaise, vinegar, Worcestershire sauce, mustard, sugar and a good pinch of salt and pepper in a large bowl. Mix well, then toss in the vegetables. Serve the chop with the slaw on the side.

PER SERVING 512 kcals, protein 32g, carbs 13g, fat 37g, sat fat 11g, fibre 4g, sugar 10g, salt 1.6g

Lemony crumbed turkey with broccoli bean smash

Lean turkey breast can easily dry out during cooking. Covering it in a crunchy, lemony crumb helps to keep it moist and imparts a zesty flavour.

TAKES 45 MINUTES • SERVES 1

1 tbsp plain flour

1 egg

25g/1oz fresh breadcrumbs

zest ½ lemon, plus lemon wedges to serve

small handful parsley, chopped

2 turkey breast steaks (about 175g/6oz in total)

1 tbsp sunflower oil

vine of cherry tomatoes

85g/3oz broccoli, cut into small florets

½ x 400g can butter beans, drained

1 tbsp pesto

1 Heat oven to 180C/160C fan/gas 4. Place the flour into a bowl with a little seasoning. Whisk the egg in a second bowl, place the breadcrumbs, lemon zest and parsley in a third bowl.

2 Dip each turkey steak into the flour, shaking off any excess, then into the egg, and finally into the breadcrumbs – press the crumbs into the turkey to make sure they really stick. Put the steaks on a large baking tray, drizzle with oil and bake for 20 minutes. Add the cherry tomatoes to the tray and bake for a further 5 minutes.

3 Meanwhile, boil a pan of water, add the broccoli and cook for 5 minutes. Add the butter beans and cook for 2 minutes, until the broccoli is tender. Drain well and leave to steam-dry for 1–2 minutes. Tip back into the pan, add the pesto and mash with a potato masher. Spoon on to a plate, with the turkey steaks, tomatoes and lemon wedges.

PER SERVING 477 kcals, protein 42g, carbs 40g, fat 17g, sat fat 3g, fibre 9g, sugar 5g, salt 1.8g

Herby lamb burger with beetroot mayo

Serve this hearty lamb burger with chunky chips as a midweek treat!

TAKES 20 MINUTES ● SERVES 1

100g/4oz minced lamb

½ small red onion, ¼ grated, ¼ thinly
  sliced

small handful parsley leaves, roughly
  chopped

small handful mint leaves, roughly
  chopped

½ tsp olive oil

1 tbsp mayonnaise

1 cooked beetroot, finely chopped

1 bread roll

handful watercress

1 Mix the lamb, grated onion and herbs in a bowl with some seasoning, then shape the mix into a burger.

2 Heat a griddle pan until hot, rub the burger with oil and cook for 5–6 minutes on each side, or until cooked through.

3 Meanwhile, mix the mayonnaise and beetroot with some seasoning. Fill the bread roll with the watercress, a burger, a dollop of beetroot mayo and a few onion slices. Serve immediately.

PER SERVING 490 kcals, protein 25g, carbs 25g, fat 32g, sat fat 9g, fibre 2g, sugar 4g, salt 1.1g

Mexican rice with chipotle pork & avocado salsa

This tasty Mexican pork dish makes a light and zingy change from the usual chilli con carne, and it will be on the table in just 30 minutes!

TAKES 30 MINUTES ● SERVES 1

140g/5oz diced pork shoulder

1 tbsp chipotle paste

1 tsp each ground cumin and smoked paprika

½ tsp sugar

½ tsp vegetable oil

50g/2oz basmati rice

½ x 400g can black beans, drained and rinsed

½ small avocado, cut into chunks

½ small red onion, finely chopped

small handful coriander leaves, roughly chopped

juice ½ lime, plus slices to squeeze over

1 tbsp pickled jalapeños slices, rinsed

1 Heat oven to 180C/160C fan/gas 4. Toss the pork with half of the chipotle paste, the cumin, paprika, sugar and some seasoning. Spread on a baking sheet, drizzle with the vegetable oil and bake for 20 minutes until tender.

2 Meanwhile, cook the rice according to the pack instructions until just cooked, then drain. Put the rice back in the pan, add the beans and keep warm with a lid on.

3 In a small bowl, toss the avocado with the red onion, most of the coriander, the remaining chipotle paste and the lime juice, then season. Serve the rice and beans with the pork, avocado salsa, jalapeños, lime slices and remaining coriander.

PER SERVING 676 kcals, protein 39g, carbs 65g, fat 28g, sat fat 7g, fibre 12g, sugar 6g, salt 0.5g

Thai-fried rice with prawns & peas

Fried rice is a great way to use up leftover veggies from the fridge. Add broccoli, peppers, corn, shredded greens or beans if you have any sitting in the veg drawer.

TAKES 20 MINUTES ● SERVES 1

2 tsp vegetable oil
½ small red onion, halved and sliced
1 small garlic clove, sliced
½ red chilli, deseeded and sliced
85g/3oz large raw prawns, peeled
85g/3oz cooked brown rice (about 40g/1½oz uncooked rice)
25g/1oz frozen peas
1 tsp dark soy sauce
1 tsp Thai fish sauce
few sprigs coriander, roughly chopped, plus a few leaves to garnish
1 egg
chilli sauce, to serve (optional)

1 Heat 1 teaspoon of the oil in a wok, add the onion, garlic and chilli, and cook for 2–3 minutes until golden. Add the prawns and cook for 1 minute. Tip in the rice and peas, and keep tossing until very hot. Add the soy and fish sauce, then stir through the chopped coriander. Keep warm while you fry the egg.

2 Heat the remaining oil in a frying pan and fry the egg with some seasoning. Tip the fried rice into a bowl and top with the fried egg. Serve scattered with the extra coriander and some chilli sauce, if you like.

PER SERVING 287 kcals, protein 22g, carbs 21g, fat 12g, sat fat 3g, fibre 3g, sugar 3g, salt 1.9g

Chicken breast with avocado salad

This healthy supper can be stuffed into a split pitta bread or warmed tortilla wrap, if you want to add some carbohydrate to the dish.

TAKES 20 MINUTES ● SERVES 1

1 boneless skinless chicken breast
2 tsp olive oil
1 heaped tsp smoked paprika

FOR THE SALAD

½ small avocado, diced
1 tsp red wine vinegar
1 tbsp parsley leaves, roughly chopped
1 medium tomato, chopped
½ small red onion, thinly sliced

1 Heat grill to medium. Rub the chicken all over with 1 teaspoon of the olive oil and the paprika. Cook for 4–5 minutes each side until lightly charred and cooked through.

2 Mix the salad ingredients together, season and add the rest of the oil. Thickly slice the chicken and serve with salad.

PER SERVING 344 kcals, protein 32g, carbs 9g, fat 20g, sat fat 4g, fibre 3g, sugar 5g, salt 0.23g

Teriyaki-chicken meatballs with rice & greens

Try a chicken dinner with a difference with these tasty patties served in a sweet Japanese sauce with basmati rice.

TAKES 25 MINUTES ● SERVES 1

1 small shallot
1 small carrot, cut into chunks
1 skinless chicken breast, cut into
    chunks
zest and juice ½ lemon
drizzle of oil, for greasing
50g/2oz basmati rice
50g/2oz spring greens, chopped
2 tbsp mirin
1 tbsp soy sauce
2 tsp caster sugar

1 Heat oven to 200C/180C fan/gas 6. Pulse the shallot and carrot in a food processor until finely chopped. Add the chicken, lemon zest and some seasoning, and pulse again until mixed. Using oiled hands, shape into small meatballs. Put on a baking sheet lined with baking parchment and bake for 10 minutes until browned and cooked through.

2 Meanwhile, boil the rice according to the pack instructions, adding the spring greens for the final 4 minutes. Drain well.

3 Add the mirin, soy, lemon juice and sugar to a pan. Bring to the boil, then simmer until saucy. Remove from the heat, add the meatballs to the pan and roll them around in the sauce. Pile the rice and greens onto a plate and spoon the meatballs over.

PER SERVING 510 kcals, protein 40g, carbs 68g, fat 4g, sat fat 1g, fibre 4g, sugar 26g, salt 3g

Crispy chilli beef

Ditch the take-away and whip up this Chinese flash-fried steak with a sweet, gingery sauce and red peppers.

TAKES 35 MINUTES • SERVES 1

100g/4oz thin-cut frying steak, very thinly sliced into strips

1 tbsp cornflour

½ tsp Chinese five-spice powder

vegetable oil, for frying

½ red pepper, deseeded and thinly sliced

½ red chilli, thinly sliced

2 spring onions, green and white parts separated, sliced

1 small garlic clove, crushed

2.5cm/1in piece ginger, peeled and cut into matchsticks

1 tbsp rice wine vinegar or white wine vinegar

½ tbsp soy sauce

1 tbsp sweet chilli sauce

1 tbsp tomato ketchup

cooked noodles, to serve (optional)

1 Put the beef in a bowl and toss in the cornflour and five spice. Heat enough oil in a wok or large frying pan to come 5cm/2in up the side of the pan. When hot add the beef and fry until golden and crisp. Scoop out the beef and drain on kitchen paper. Pour away all but a drizzle of oil.

2 Add the pepper, half the chilli, the white ends of the spring onions, garlic and ginger to the pan. Stir-fry for 3 minutes to soften, but don't let the garlic and ginger burn. Mix the vinegar, soy, chilli sauce and ketchup in a jug with 2 tablespoons water, then pour over the veg. Bubble for 2 minutes, then add the beef back to the pan and toss well to coat. Serve the beef on noodles, if you like, scattered with the remaining chilli and the green parts of the spring onions.

PER SERVING 375 kcals, protein 23g, carbs 31g, fat 18g, sat fat 4g, fibre 3g, sugar 17g, salt 2.7g

Herby pork with apple & chicory salad

To make this recipe you'll have to buy a whole pork tenderloin, but you can cut it into individual portions and freeze any you're not using for another day.

TAKES 35 MINUTES • SERVES 1

140g/5oz piece pork tenderloin, trimmed of any fat and sinew
2 tsp walnut oil
1 tsp wholegrain mustard
1 tsp each chopped tarragon and parsley leaves
squeeze lemon juice
1 tsp clear honey
½ small crunchy apple, cored and sliced
1 head chicory, leaves separated

1 Heat oven to 200C/180C fan/gas 6. Rub the pork with 1 teaspoon of the oil, ½ teaspoon of the mustard and some seasoning. Quickly brown in a small pan, then transfer to a baking sheet and press on half the herbs. Roast for 10 minutes until just cooked.

2 To make the salad, mix the lemon juice, honey and remaining walnut oil and mustard together. Season and toss through the apple, chicory and remaining herbs. Serve the pork sliced, with the salad on the side.

PER SERVING 215 kcals, protein 23g, carbs 15g, fat 8g, sat fat 2g, fibre 2g, sugar 14g, salt 0.3g

Chicken, butter bean & pepper stew

The perfect one-pan supper; chuck all the ingredients in then leave to bubble while you get on with other things. Serve with crusty bread to soak up the sauce.

TAKES 1 HOUR ● SERVES 1

1 tsp olive oil
1 shallot, chopped
1 celery stick, chopped
1 yellow or red pepper, or a mix of
    both, deseeded and diced
1 small garlic clove, crushed
1 tsp sweet paprika
200g can chopped tomatoes
75ml/3fl oz chicken stock
½ x 400g can butter beans, drained
    and rinsed
2 skinless chicken thighs, bone-in
crusty bread, to serve (optional)

1 Heat oven to 180C/160C fan/gas 4. Heat the oil in a large flameproof casserole dish. Add the shallot, celery and pepper, and fry for 5 minutes. Add the garlic and paprika, and cook for a further 3 minutes.
2 Stir in the tomatoes, stock and butter beans, and season well. Bring to the boil, then nestle the chicken thighs into the sauce. Cover with a tight-fitting lid and put in the oven for 45 minutes. Spoon into a bowl and eat with crusty bread, if you like.

PER SERVING 422 kcals, protein 44g, carbs 27g, fat 15g, sat fat 4g, fibre 9g, sugar 12g, salt 1.6g

Steamed fish with ginger & spring onion

Steaming the fish in a parcel really locks in all the flavour from the ginger and spring onions – better still, it will save you some washing up!

TAKES 20 MINUTES • SERVES 1

1 pak choi, leaves separated
140g/5oz firm white fish fillet
few slices ginger, finely shredded
1 small garlic clove, finely sliced
2 tsp low-salt soy sauce
1 tsp mirin
3 spring onions, finely shredded
few sprigs coriander, chopped
lime wedges, to squeeze over
boiled brown rice, to serve

1 Heat oven to 200C/180C fan/gas 6. Cut a large rectangle of foil, big enough to make a large envelope. Put the pak choi on the foil, followed by the fish, then the ginger and garlic. Pour over the soy sauce and mirin, then season.

2 Fold over the foil and seal the three edges, then put on a baking sheet. Cook for 20 minutes, open the parcel and scatter over the spring onions and coriander. Serve with the lime wedges to squeeze over and the brown rice.

PER SERVING 145 kcals, protein 29g, carbs 4g, fat 1g, sat fat none, fibre 1g, sugar 3g, salt 1.1g

Miso–chilli steak with crispy sweet potatoes

This Asian-inspired version of steak and chips uses miso paste to flavour the steak.
Miso paste is made from soya beans and imparts a lovely savoury, umami flavour.

TAKES 30 MINUTES • SERVES 1

1 large sweet potato, cut into wedges
½ tbsp vegetable oil, plus a little extra
   for the steak
2 tsp sesame seeds
½ tbsp miso paste
juice ½ lemon
½ tbsp hot chilli sauce (Sriracha is nice)
½ tbsp mirin
1 bavette or other lean steak (about
   200g/7oz)
handful watercress, to garnish

1 Heat oven to 200C/180C fan/gas 6.
Put the potato wedges on a baking sheet
and rub with the oil. Sprinkle over the
sesame seeds and some seasoning.
Bake for 25 minutes or until crisp at
the edges.

2 In a small bowl, mix together the
miso, lemon juice, chilli sauce and mirin.
Rub the steak with a tiny bit of oil and
some seasoning. Spoon 1 tablespoon of
the sauce over the steak and rub into
both sides.

3 Heat a griddle pan until really hot,
cook the steak for 2 minutes each side,
or longer if you prefer it well done. Brush
more of the sauce over after you turn
it. Transfer to a plate, cover loosely with
foil and leave to rest for 5 minutes.
Serve the steak sliced, with the
remaining sauce, the potato wedges
and watercress.

PER SERVING 582 kcals, protein 47g, carbs 47g,
fat 23g, sat fat 7g, fibre 8g, sugar 16g, salt 1.1g

Chicken cacciatore

Once tasted, this super-easy take on a Good Food *favourite is sure to become a regular in your home too.*

TAKES 55 MINUTES • SERVES 1

1 small shallot, sliced
1 garlic clove, sliced
1 tsp olive oil
200g can chopped tomatoes
1 tsp chopped rosemary leaves
1 chicken breast
few basil leaves, to garnish
favourite seasonal vegetables,
   to serve (optional)
mashed cannellini beans,
   to serve (optional)

1 Fry the shallot and garlic in the oil until softened. Add the tomatoes, rosemary and some seasoning, and cook for 10–15 minutes until thickened.
2 Heat oven to 180C/160C fan/gas 4. Put the chicken in a small baking dish, top with the sauce and bake for 15–20 minutes until cooked through. Serve scattered with basil and with your favourite seasonal veg and mashed cannellini beans or potatoes, if you like.

PER SERVING 171 kcals, protein 32g, carbs 6g, fat 2g, sat fat 1g, fibre 2g, sugar 4g, salt 0.3g

Black bean beef meatballs with stir-fried noodles

Try this new take on a stir fry which uses beef meatballs and a sweet and sticky black-bean sauce.

TAKES 45 MINUTES • SERVES 1

85g/3oz minced beef
25g/1oz fresh breadcrumbs
2 tbsp black bean sauce
1 tbsp tomato ketchup
1 tbsp sweet chilli sauce
½ tsp Chinese five-spice powder
1 nest medium egg noodles
1 tsp sunflower oil
small pack mixed stir-fry vegetables
1 tbsp soy sauce
1 tsp sesame seeds
few mint leaves, to garnish

1 Heat oven to 220C/200C fan/gas 7. Make the meatballs by mixing together the minced beef, breadcrumbs, half the black bean sauce, ketchup and sweet chilli sauce and ¼ teaspoon of the five-spice. Shape the mix into walnut-sized meatballs. Transfer to a baking sheet in a single layer and cook for 25 minutes, turning once, until golden brown.

2 Meanwhile, cook the noodles according to the pack instructions, drain and set aside. Heat the oil in a wok or large frying pan. Cook the vegetables in the oil for a few minutes, then add the noodles and remaining black bean, sweet chilli, ketchup, five-spice and the soy sauce, tossing well to coat everything.

3 Tip the noodles and vegetables into a serving bowl, top with the meatballs and sprinkle with the sesame seeds and mint.

PER SERVING 639 kcals, protein 30g, carbs 87g, fat 19g, sat fat 6g, fibre 5g, sugar 18g, salt 5.1g

Minced-beef pie with minty mushy peas

This comforting pie really hits the spot on a chilly evening; serve with mashed potato and gravy to really up the comfort factor!

TAKES 1 HOUR • SERVES 1

1 shallot, chopped
2 carrots, chopped
1 small celery stick, chopped
1 tsp olive oil
140g/5oz lean minced beef
2 tsp tomato purée
1 tsp Worcestershire sauce
100ml/3½fl oz beef stock
1 egg yolk, lightly beaten
100g/4oz ready-rolled puff pastry
100g/4oz frozen peas
1 tsp mint sauce

1 Fry the onion, carrots and celery in the oil in a large frying pan until softened. Add the mince, increase the heat and cook for 5 minutes or until well browned. Stir in the tomato purée, Worcestershire sauce and stock. Simmer for 5 minutes until the sauce has thickened slightly. Cool for 10 minutes.

2 Heat oven to 200C/180C fan/gas 6. Spoon the mixture into a small pie dish. Brush the rim with some of the beaten egg yolk, then lay the pastry on top and trim. Seal the edges with a fork and brush the pastry with more egg yolk. Poke a little hole in the top and cook for 25–30 minutes or until the pastry is golden and risen.

3 Meanwhile, cook the peas in boiling water, then drain and mash with the mint sauce. Serve the pie with the hot peas on the side.

PER SERVING 731 kcals, protein 10g, carbs 51g, fat 39g, sat fat 17g, fibre 8g, sugar 14g, salt 1.6g

Sausage casserole with quick garlic bread

This tasty one-pot is perfect served with homemade garlic bread for soaking up the tomatoey sauce.

TAKES 40 MINUTES • SERVES 1

1 tsp olive oil, plus extra for drizzling
2 sausages
½ onion, sliced
1 carrot, finely chopped
1 celery sticks, finely chopped
200g/7oz cherry tomatoes (canned or fresh)
½ x 400g can cannellini beans, undrained
½ beef stock cube
1½ tsp thyme leaves, chopped, plus extra for garlic bread
1 garlic clove, ½ grated, ½ whole
1 small ciabatta roll

1 Heat the oil in a wide, shallow pan with a lid and fry the sausages until browned. Push to one side, then tip in the onion, carrot and celery, and cook, with the lid on, for 10 minutes until softened.

2 Stir in the tomatoes, beans and their juice, the stock cube and thyme. Add the grated garlic, cover and simmer for 10 minutes.

3 Meanwhile, toast the ciabatta, then rub with the remaining garlic, drizzle with the extra oil, scatter with the few extra thyme leaves and serve with the casserole.

PER SERVING 701 kcals, protein 29g, carbs 71g, fat 34g, sat fat 11g, fibre 8g, sugar 20g, salt 5.3g

All-in-one gammon, egg & chips

Save washing-up – and the pennies – with this easy one-pan dish. Add a ring of pineapple for a retro garnish.

TAKES 50 MINUTES • SERVES 1

1 large baking potato, unpeeled, cut
    into chunky chips
1 tsp olive oil
1 small gammon steak
1 egg
tomato ketchup, to serve (optional)

1 Heat oven to 200C/180C fan/gas 6. Drizzle the potato chips with the oil and some salt and pepper. Bake in a roasting tin for 25 minutes, until starting to go brown.
2 Remove and turn the chips. Push to the edges of the tin, put the gammon in the centre and cook for 7 minutes more. Take the tin out of the oven and turn the gammon over, then crack the egg into a corner of the tin. Cook for 7 minutes more until the egg is set and the gammon is cooked through. Serve with ketchup, if you like.

PER SERVING 581 kcals, protein 37g, carbs 34g, fat 34g, sat fat 11g, fibre 3g, sugar 1g, salt 4.82g

Ham & ricotta pizza with pesto

Ditch the take-away – this easy pizza uses only six ingredients and will be on the table in half an hour!

TAKES 30 MINUTES ● SERVES 1

2 tbsp tomato pasta sauce
1 small pizza base
1 slice ham, roughly torn
50g/2oz ricotta
1 tbsp fresh pesto
few basil leaves, to garnish

1 Heat oven to 220C/200C fan/gas 7. Put a baking sheet in the oven to heat up. Meanwhile, spread the tomato sauce on the pizza base. Carefully slide the base on to the baking sheet and cook according to the pack instructions.
2 Just 5 minutes before the cooking time is up, scatter over the ham, dot the ricotta on top in spoonfuls and return the pizza to the oven. When the top is bubbling and the base is turning brown, remove from the oven, season then drizzle the pesto over each pizza and scatter with basil before serving.

PER SERVING 282 kcals, protein 13g, carbs 43g, fat 7g, sat fat 3g, fibre 1g, sugar 4g, salt 1.51g

Pork Milanese with spaghetti

This classic dish can be made with pork, chicken or, more traditionally, veal. The piquant sauce cuts through the richness of the breadcrumbed meat beautifully.

TAKES 45 MINUTES ● SERVES 1

1 tsp olive oil
1 small garlic clove, crushed
200g can chopped tomatoes
1 tsp balsamic vinegar
1 large or 2 small pork steaks, fat and
    bone removed
1 tbsp plain flour
1 egg, beaten
25g/1oz fresh breadcrumbs
100g/4oz spaghetti
few basil leaves, torn

1 Heat the oil in a pan, then fry the garlic for a few seconds. Add the chopped tomatoes and balsamic vinegar, and bubble for about 10 minutes until the sauce is thick. Keep warm and set aside.
2 Meanwhile, lay the pork between two layers of cling film and bash with a rolling pin until about 1cm/½in thick. Mix the flour with some seasoning in one bowl, put the egg in another and the breadcrumbs in a third. Dip the pork in the flour, then the egg, then the breadcrumbs. Heat a grill to hot, then cook the pork for 3 minutes on each side, until golden and cooked through. Keep warm.
3 Cook the pasta according to the pack instructions. Stir through the tomato sauce and the torn basil, transfer to a plate, put the crispy pork on top and eat immediately.

PER SERVING 759 kcals, protein 47g, carbs 109g, fat 15g, sat fat 4g, fibre 6g, sugar 10g, salt 1g

Chorizo, potato & cheese omelette

Spruce up a regular cheese omelette with the addition of paprika-slicked chorizo and boiled potatoes. Serve with a salad for an easy and delicious supper.

TAKES 30 MINUTES ● MAKES 1

1 small potato, cut into 2.5cm/1in dice
1 tsp olive oil
50g/2oz cooking chorizo, chopped
2–3 eggs
small handful parsley leaves, chopped
25g/1oz grated Cheddar

1 Cook the potato in boiling water for 8–10 minutes or until tender. Drain and allow to steam-dry.
2 Heat the oil in an omelette pan, add the chorizo and cook for 2 minutes. Add the potato and cook for a further 5 minutes until it starts to crisp.
3 Spoon out the pan contents, wipe the pan and cook a 2- or 3-egg omelette in the same pan. When almost cooked, scatter with the chorizo and potato, parsley and cheese. Fold the omelette in the pan and cook for 1 minute more to melt the cheese before serving straight away.

PER OMLETTE 602 kcals, protein 36g, carbs 15g, fat 44g, sat fat 18g, fibre 1g, sugar 2g, salt 1.8g

Sausages with warm red-cabbage & beetroot slaw

Hot dogs are brought up to date with the crunchy beetroot slaw – perfect for a Friday night in front of the TV!

TAKES 45 MINUTES ● SERVES 1

2 pork sausages
2 tbsp balsamic vinegar
2 tbsp dark soft brown sugar
1 tsp cumin seeds
25g/1oz mixed dried vine fruit, such as
    currants, raisins and sultanas
¼ small red cabbage, shredded
1 beetroot, grated
chunk of baguette and English mustard,
    to serve

1 Heat oven to 200C/180C fan/gas 6. Put the sausages on a baking tray and cook for 30–35 minutes or until cooked through and golden.

2 Meanwhile, put the vinegar, sugar, cumin and dried fruit into a large pan, and gently heat until the sugar dissolves. Bring to the boil, then bubble for 1 minute or until slightly reduced. Tip in the cabbage and beetroot, stir well, then cook for 10 minutes more.

3 Serve as a hot dog in a chunk of baguette with the warm slaw and a little mustard.

PER SERVING 632 kcals, protein 18g, carbs 11g, fat 29g, sat fat 10g, fibre 10g, sugar 69g, salt 2.7g

Hot salami & courgette flatbread

Turn a humble wrap into something special. You can swap the courgettes for thinly sliced aubergine or peppers, if you have some lying around in the fridge.

TAKES 20 MINUTES ● SERVES 1

1 small courgette, thinly sliced
2 tsp olive oil
pinch dried or fresh oregano
1 flatbread or Mediterranean wrap
2 tbsp chilli and tomato pasta sauce
2 slices salami, cut into strips
25g/1oz Emmental or Cheddar, grated

1 Heat oven to 220C/200C fan/gas 7 and put a griddle pan on the hob over a high heat. Toss the courgette slices in a bowl with the olive oil, oregano and some seasoning. Lay the courgette slices on the griddle and cook for a few minutes each side until just tender.

2 Put the flatbread or wrap on a baking sheet and spread with the pasta sauce. Arrange the courgette slices on top, before scattering over the salami and cheese.

3 Put the flatbread or wrap in the oven and bake for 8 minutes until the cheese has melted and the edges of the base are crisp and golden.

PER SERVING 355 kcals, protein 17g, carbs 31g, fat 19g, sat fat 7g, fibre 2g, sugar 5g, salt 1.6g

Quick bean & chorizo chilli

This simple chilli is easily doubled and makes a great jacket-potato filling for another day.

TAKES 20 MINUTES • SERVES 1

50g/2oz cooking chorizo, sliced

200g can chopped tomatoes

1 tbsp harissa paste

½ x 400g can kidney beans, drained and rinsed

½ x 400g can chickpeas, drained and rinsed

rice and natural yogurt, or jacket potatoes and soured cream, to serve

1 Dry-fry the chorizo for a few minutes in a non-stick frying pan until crisp. Carefully pour off any fat from the pan, then tip in the tomatoes, harissa, beans and chickpeas with 50ml/2fl oz water. Bring to a simmer, cover, then lower the heat and bubble for 10 minutes.

2 Spoon over rice or a jacket potato and serve with yogurt or soured cream.

PER SERVING 463 kcals, protein 29g, carbs 50g, fat 18g, sat fat 6g, fibre 17g, sugar 17g, salt 6.32g

Sundried tomato & bacon spaghetti

The sundried tomato pesto in the pasta sauce packs in loads of rich flavour; serve scattered with Parmesan, if you like.

TAKES 25 MINUTES • SERVES 1

100g/4oz spaghetti
1 tsp olive oil
1 small carrot, finely diced
1 small celery stick, finely diced
50g/2oz smoked bacon lardons
3 tbsp sundried tomato pesto
few basil leaves, shredded (optional)

1 Boil the spaghetti according to the pack instructions. Meanwhile, heat the oil in a non-stick pan. Add the carrot, celery and bacon, and stir well. Cover the pan and cook, stirring occasionally, for 10 minutes until the veg has softened.
2 Tip in the pesto, warm through, then stir through the drained spaghetti with the basil, if using, and serve.

PER SERVING 694 kcals, protein 24g, carbs 81g, fat 31g, sat fat 7g, fibre 7g, sugar 11g, salt 2.1g

Raid-the-cupboard tuna & sweetcorn cake

The classic combo of tuna and sweetcorn is brought up to date in this chunky fishcake – serve with mayo and chips, if you fancy a treat.

TAKES 30 MINUTES ● SERVES 1

100g/4oz potatoes, quartered
1 tbsp mayonnaise, plus extra to serve
100g/4oz canned tuna, drained and
    flaked
50g/2oz canned sweetcorn, drained
few chives, snipped
1 egg, beaten
25g/1oz dried breadcrumbs
sunflower oil, for frying
salad and your favourite dressing,
    to serve

1 Cook the potatoes in boiling salted water until really tender. Drain and allow to steam-dry in a colander. Tip into a bowl, season and mash. Stir in the mayonnaise, tuna, sweetcorn and chives. Shape into a chunky fishcake and chill until cold and firm.

2 Dip the fishcake into the egg, letting the excess drip off, then coat in the breadcrumbs. Chill for 15 minutes.

3 Heat a little oil in a pan and gently fry the cake for 2–3 minutes on each side until golden. Serve with an extra dollop of mayonnaise and dressed salad leaves alongside.

PER CAKE 467 kcals, protein 27g, carbs 42g, fat 22g, sat fat 3g, fibre 3g, sugar 4g, salt 1.3g

Chorizo–bean burger

Treat yourself to this spicy sausage-and-bean burger, and make extra patties to stash in the freezer if you like.

TAKES 25 MINUTES ● SERVES 1

50g/2oz mini cooking chorizo, skins removed

2 pork sausages, squeezed from their skins

pinch smoked paprika

2 tsp lime juice, plus wedges to serve

small handful coriander leaves, chopped

½ x 200g can mixed beans, drained and rinsed

1 medium egg, beaten

1 tbsp olive oil, plus extra to drizzle

1 ciabatta roll, split and toasted

soured cream, avocado slices, small handful rocket leaves and chips, to serve

1 In a food processor, pulse the chorizo, sausage meat, paprika, lime juice and coriander until well combined. Add the beans and some seasoning, and quickly pulse again to mix. Tip into a bowl and mix in just enough egg to bind. Shape into a fat burger, cover and chill for 15 minutes. Heat oven to 200C/180C fan/gas 6.

2 Heat the oil in a pan and fry the burger for 3 minutes on each side. Transfer to a baking sheet and cook in the oven for a further 10 minutes until cooked through.

3 Serve the burger in a roll with soured cream, avocado and rocket, with chips and a lime wedge on the side, if you like.

PER SERVING 710 kcals, protein 32g, carbs 18g, fat 56g, sat fat 18g, fibre 5g, sugar 5g, salt 3.3g

Shepherd's pie potatoes

Jacket potatoes just got a makeover – pile the fluffy mash on top of the meaty sauce for a warming supper for one.

TAKES 1 HOUR ● SERVES 1

2 tsp butter
1 shallot, chopped
140g/5oz lean minced beef
250ml/9fl oz beef stock
1 tsp Worcestershire sauce
1 tbsp tomato purée
1 large jacket potato, baked
small handful grated Cheddar
your favourite veg, to serve

1 Heat oven to 200C/180C fan/gas 6. Melt half the butter in a non-stick pan. Cook the shallot for 3–4 minutes, then increase the heat and add the mince. Fry for a further 3–4 minutes until the beef has browned. Stir in the stock, Worcestershire sauce, tomato purée and some seasoning. Gently bubble for 15–20 minutes until the mince is tender and the sauce has thickened.

2 To assemble, cut the jacket potato in half lengthways and scoop the flesh into a small bowl, leaving the skin intact. Mash the potato flesh with the remaining butter and season well. Divide the mince between the potato skins, then cover with the mash. Transfer the potatoes to a baking dish, sprinkle with cheese, then bake for 15–20 minutes until golden. Serve with your favourite veg.

PER SERVING 779 kcals, protein 50g, carbs 79g, fat 31g, sat fat 15g, fibre 7g, sugar 9g, salt 2.43g

Lamb kebabs & Greek salad

Look out for lean cuts of lamb for these kebabs and make sure you trim any excess fat or sinew before cooking.

TAKES 30 MINUTES • SERVES 1

squeeze lemon juice
2 tsp olive oil
1 small garlic clove, crushed
140g/5oz diced lamb leg

FOR THE SALAD

1 large tomato, chopped
5cm/2in piece cucumber, chopped
5 pitted black olives, roughly chopped
50g/2oz feta, crumbled
few mint leaves, chopped

1 Mix the lemon juice, olive oil and garlic in a mixing bowl. Pour half into a jug and set aside for later. Add the lamb to the bowl, stir to coat, then thread on to two small skewers; if using wooden skewers, soak them in water for at least 30 minutes before use. Leave to stand for 10 minutes.

2 Meanwhile, mix all the salad ingredients together, except the mint, and pour over the reserved lemon juice and oil mix.

3 Heat a griddle pan. Cook the lamb for 8 minutes, turning every couple of minutes, until cooked through and slightly charred. Mix the mint through the salad and serve immediately with the kebabs.

PER SERVING 495 kcals, protein 38g, carbs 5g, fat 36g, sat fat 16g, fibre 2g, sugar 4g, salt 2.2g

Fish fingers with mushy peas

We all love this school days' classic, and the homemade version is much better than frozen options. Double the amount and save half for a fish finger butty the next day!

TAKES 25 MINUTES • SERVES 1

140g/5oz sustainable firm skinless white fish fillets, such as pollack or hake
1–2 tbsp plain flour, seasoned
1 egg, beaten
50g/2oz fresh breadcrumbs
2 tsp vegetable oil
100g/4oz frozen peas
knob butter
zest ½ lemon, zested lemon cut into wedges to squeeze over
few mint leaves, finely chopped
new potatoes, to serve

1 Slice the fish into fingers, each about 2.5cm/1in thick. Put the seasoned flour, egg and breadcrumbs into three separate shallow bowls. Dust the fish pieces first in the flour, then coat well in the egg and cover completely in the breadcrumbs. Put the coated fish on a plate and chill for 15 minutes.

2 Heat the oil in a large frying pan. Add the fish fingers and fry for 8 minutes, turning occasionally, until golden and cooked through. Meanwhile, add the peas to a small pan of boiling water. Cook for 4 minutes until really tender. Drain, tip into a bowl with the butter, zest and mint, and roughly mash with a potato masher. Season to taste and keep warm.

3 Serve the golden fish fingers with a generous spoonful of mushy peas, lemon wedges and new potatoes, if you like.

PER SERVING 489 kcals, protein 42g, carbs 55g, fat 11g, sat fat 2g, fibre 9g, sugar 5g, salt 1.3g

Roasted onion & bacon salad

Make this thrifty salad from leftover ingredients in your fridge.

TAKES 30 MINUTES ● SERVES 1

1 red onion, cut into 8 wedges, root left
   intact
2 tbsp olive oil, plus extra for drizzling
   (optional)
handful peas (fresh or frozen)
1 tsp sherry vinegar
1 tsp Dijon mustard
2 rashers smoked streaky bacon
1 slice bread, cut into cubes
1 Baby Gem lettuce, leaves torn

1 Heat oven to 220C/200C fan/gas 7. Arrange the onion wedges on one side of a baking sheet. Drizzle with ½ tablespoon of the olive oil and season. Put in the oven and roast for 15 minutes.
2 Meanwhile, cook the peas in boiling water for 2 minutes, then drain and rinse in very cold water. Set aside.
3 Make the dressing by mixing together another ½ tablespoon of the oil, the vinegar, mustard and some seasoning. Turn the onions and put the bacon rashers and bread alongside on the baking sheet. Drizzle the remaining oil over the bread. Return the sheet to the oven for 12 minutes more, until golden.
4 Put the lettuce and peas in a bowl, add the dressing and toss to combine. Arrange the onion and bread on top. Break up the bacon slightly and scatter over. Drizzle with a little more olive oil, if you like, and eat straight away.

PER SERVING 498 kcals, protein 14g, carbs 27g, fat 37g, sat fat 7g, fibre 8g, sugar 12g, salt 2.3g

Sausage & mash pie

If you have a pack of 8 sausages, make four pies and store them in the freezer for up to 2 months. Otherwise buy sausages individually from the butcher to prevent waste.

TAKES 1 HOUR 5 MINUTES ● SERVES 1

250g/9oz potatoes, cut into even
   chunks
small knob butter
1 tbsp milk
small wedge (about 20g/1oz) Red
   Leicester or Cheddar, finely diced
1 tsp sunflower oil
1 shallot, chopped
2 large meaty pork & leek sausages,
   removed from their skins
50ml/2fl oz chicken stock
1 small tomato, cut into 6 wedges
veg of your choice or baked beans,
   to serve

1 Heat oven to 200C/180C fan/gas 6. Boil the potatoes for 20 minutes, then drain and mash with the butter, milk and some seasoning. Stir in the Red Leicester or Cheddar.

2 Meanwhile, heat the oil in a non-stick pan and fry the shallot, stirring frequently, for 5 minutes until softened. Add the sausages and break them up with a wooden spoon until you get a texture similar to chunky mince. Pour in the stock and simmer for 8 minutes.

3 Spoon the sausage mixture into an individual pie dish. Top with the cheesy mash. You can bake the pie now or freeze for up to 2 months; simply thaw in the fridge before baking. Bake for 25–30 minutes until starting to turn golden. Top with the tomato wedges and serve with your favourite veg or some baked beans.

PER PIE 728 kcals, protein 27g, carbs 56g, fat 44g, sat fat 19g, fibre 6g, sugar 10g, salt 3.1g

Baked eggs with spinach & ham

Serve this versatile Mexican-style dish for brunch, lunch or supper, with lots of crusty bread for dunking.

TAKES 40 MINUTES • SERVES 1

1 tsp olive oil
1 small shallot, finely chopped
1 small garlic clove, crushed
½ small green chilli, deseeded and
    finely chopped
200g can chopped tomatoes
2 ready-roasted peppers from a jar,
    drained and sliced
75g/2½oz ham, torn, or shredded ham
    hock
handful baby leaf spinach
2 medium eggs
pinch cayenne pepper
crusty bread, to serve

1 Heat oven to 180C/160C fan/gas 4. Heat the oil in a small ovenproof pan. Add the shallot and cook for 6 minutes until softened. Stir in the garlic and chilli, and cook for a couple of minutes more.

2 Add the tomatoes and 50ml/2fl oz water. Season well and stir through the peppers and ham. Bring to a simmer and cook for 10 minutes until the sauce has started to thicken. Add the spinach, stirring through to wilt.

3 Make two hollows in the sauce and crack in the eggs. Add a pinch of cayenne, transfer to the oven and bake for 10 minutes until the whites of the eggs have set. Serve straight away with crusty bread.

PER SERVING 325 kcals, protein 32g, carbs 11g, fat 18g, sat fat 5g, fibre 4g, sugar 7g, salt 2.7g

Minced beef & sweet potato stew

This healthy stew is easily doubled or quadrupled and freezes really well. Make extra portions and freeze for up to 2 months for a speedy and healthy dinner.

TAKES 1 HOUR 20 MINUTES
- **SERVES 1**

1 tbsp sunflower oil
½ small onion, chopped
1 small carrot, chopped
½ small celery stick, sliced
140g/5oz lean minced beef
1 tsp tomato purée
100g/4oz chopped tomatoes (from a can)
1 sweet potato, peeled and cut into large chunks
1 thyme sprig
1 bay leaf
small handful parsley leaves, chopped
steamed Savoy cabbage, to serve

1 Heat the oil in a large pan, add the onion, carrot and celery, and sweat for 10 minutes until soft. Add the beef and cook until it is browned all over.

2 Add the tomato purée and cook for a few minutes, then add the tomatoes, sweet potato, herbs and a can full of water. Season well and bring to the boil.

3 Simmer for 40–45 minutes on a low heat until the sweet potatoes are tender, stirring a few times throughout cooking to make sure they are cooking evenly.

4 Once cooked, remove the bay leaf, stir through the chopped parsley and serve with steamed cabbage.

PER SERVING 368 kcals, protein 29g, carbs 35g, fat 13g, sat fat 5g, fibre 6g, sugar 17g, salt 0.6g

Sardine storecupboard spaghetti

Rich in omega-3 and omega-6 oils, canned sardines are an excellent source of vitamin D, calcium and phosphorous.

TAKES 20 MINUTES ● SERVES 1

100g/4oz spaghetti
1 tbsp olive oil
1 shallot, finely chopped
2 large garlic cloves, finely chopped
10 cherry tomatoes, halved
95g can boneless sardines in olive oil, drained
8 pitted green olives, halved
2 tsp capers
handful parsley leaves, chopped

1 Cook the spaghetti according to the pack instructions. Meanwhile, heat the oil in a pan, tip in the shallot and cook for 5 minutes or until soft. Add the garlic and tomatoes, and cook for a few minutes more.

2 Stir through the sardines, breaking them up lightly with the back of a spoon. Add the olives and capers, then season and heat through. Toss in the cooked, drained spaghetti, a splash of the pasta cooking water and the chopped parsley. Serve immediately.

PER SERVING 801 kcals, protein 38g, carbs 82g, fat 36g, sat fat 6g, fibre 12g, sugar 11g, salt 2.4g

Cheesy–eggy bread with chunky salad

For perfect eggy bread, leave the bread to soak up the cheesy egg mixture for a few minutes before cooking. You'll get lovely puffed-up eggy bread.

TAKES 20 MINUTES • SERVES 1

knob of butter and a drizzle of oil, for frying (optional)
2 medium eggs, beaten
50g/2oz Cheddar, very finely grated
2 chunky slices bread from a small crusty loaf, or 3 from a baguette

FOR THE SALAD

handful cherry tomatoes, halved
½ avocado, diced
chunk cucumber, diced
small handful rocket leaves

1 Heat a good non-stick frying pan (if you don't have one, heat a normal pan with a knob of butter and drizzle of oil). Whisk the eggs and cheese with some seasoning in a shallow dish. Lay the bread in so it soaks up a little egg. Flip over and leave to soak for 1 minute more, or until most of the egg mixture has been soaked up. Scoop out any cheese from the dish, pressing it to stick on to the bread. Fry for 2–4 minutes on each side until golden.

2 Mix the salad ingredients together with some seasoning and serve alongside.

PER SERVING 657 kcals, protein 36g, carbs 33g, fat 46g, sat fat 17g, fibre 5g, sugar 4g, salt 2.28g

Squash risotto

Use butternut squash for this tasty supper, or if you can find a small sweet pumpkin or onion squash when in season, this will lend a lovely flavour to the dish.

TAKES 45 MINUTES ● SERVES 1

100g pack chopped butternut squash or pumpkin

1 tsp olive oil, plus a drizzle for the squash or pumpkin

small knob butter

2 spring onions, chopped

1 small garlic clove, crushed

50g/2oz risotto rice

½ tsp ground cumin

250ml/9fl oz hot vegetable stock, plus extra splash if needed

Parmesan (or vegetarian alternative) grated, to taste

few coriander leaves, roughly chopped

1 Heat oven to 180C/160C fan/gas 4. Put the squash or pumpkin on a baking sheet, drizzle over some oil, then roast for 30 minutes.

2 Meanwhile, make the risotto. Heat the oil with the butter in a pan over a medium heat. Add the spring onions and garlic. Once the onions are soft but not getting brown, add the rice and cumin. Stir well to coat in the buttery mix for about 1 minute.

3 Now add half a cup of the stock, and stir every now and then until it has all disappeared into the rice. Carry on adding and stirring in a large splash of stock at a time, until you have used up all the stock – this will take 20 minutes.

4 Check the rice is cooked. If it isn't, add a splash more stock, and carry on cooking for a bit longer. Once the rice is soft enough to eat, gently stir in some grated cheese, chopped coriander and the roasted squash.

PER SERVING 397 kcals, protein 18g, carbs 47g, fat 14g, sat fat 7g, fibre 5g, sugar 6g, salt 1g

Cheesy beans & sweetcorn cakes with quick salsa

You'll find most of the ingredients for these corn cakes in the storecupboard. If you have a jar of salsa in the cupboard you can serve them with this too.

TAKES 25 MINUTES • SERVES 1

200g can chickpeas, drained and rinsed
50g/2oz canned sweetcorn, drained
25g/1oz mature Cheddar, grated
2–6 (depending on how hot you like it) jalapeño chilli slices from a jar, finely chopped
1 egg yolk, beaten
small handful coriander leaves, chopped
1 tbsp vegetable oil
5 cherry tomatoes, quartered
½ small red onion, sliced
juice ½ lime
mixed salad leaves, to serve (optional)

1 Put the chickpeas and half the sweetcorn in the bowl of a food processor and blend until smooth or mash with a fork. Tip into a bowl and add the cheese, jalapeños, egg yolk, half the coriander and the remaining sweetcorn. Season, mix well to combine, then shape into eight patties.

2 Heat the oil in a large frying pan and cook the patties for 4 minutes on each side until brown and crisp.

3 Mix the tomatoes, onion, remaining coriander and the lime juice with a little salt to make a salsa. Serve the cakes with the salsa and some salad leaves, if you like.

PER SERVING 492 kcals, protein 21g, carbs 36g, fat 30g, sat fat 9g, fibre 9g, sugar 10g, salt 1.5g

Butternut squash, spinach & feta filo pie

A healthy pie that contains two of your 5-a-day, this is sure to become a firm favourite.

TAKES 1 HOUR ● SERVES 1

250g/9oz butternut squash, peeled, deseeded and cut into 2.5cm/1in dice (prepared weight)
½ red onion, cut into wedges
pinch chilli flakes
100g/4oz fresh or frozen spinach leaves
25g/1oz feta, crumbled
1 sheet filo pastry
1 tsp olive oil
green salad, to serve (optional)

1 Heat oven to 220C/200C fan/gas 7. Put the squash, onion and chilli flakes in a small, ovenproof pie dish. Season and cook for 20 minutes until the squash is tender and the onions are starting to char at the edges.

2 Meanwhile, put the spinach in a colander and pour over a kettleful of boiling water (if using frozen spinach, allow to defrost before using). Squeeze out any excess liquid and stir into the squash mix. Dot over the feta, crumple up the pastry and put on top, then brush with the oil. Return to the oven and cook for a further 15 minutes until the pastry is golden and crisp. Serve with a green salad, if you like.

PER SERVING 294 kcals, protein 12g, carbs 40g, fat 10g, sat fat 4g, fibre 8g, sugar 17g, salt 1.4g

Spicy courgette pitta pocket

Courgettes are one of the most loved veggies in the UK, so why not try something a little different with them tonight?

TAKES 15 MINUTES ● SERVES 1

1 courgette, thinly sliced lengthways
2 tsp harissa paste
2 tsp olive oil
small handful broad beans (fresh or
   frozen)
2 tbsp houmous
1 spring onion, finely sliced
1 tsp tahini paste
small garlic clove, crushed
squeeze lemon juice
1 tbsp Greek-style yogurt
1 large wholemeal pitta

1 Toss the courgette slices in the harissa and olive oil, and season. Cook on a hot griddle pan for 2 minutes each side or until tender. Transfer to a plate and set aside.

2 Cook the broad beans in boiling water for 2 minutes, drain under cold running water, then slip them out of their outer skins. Discard the skins. Put the broad beans, houmous and spring onion in a small bowl, and mix to combine.

3 In another bowl, mix the tahini, garlic, lemon juice and yogurt. Toast the pitta and split it to create two pockets. Spoon the houmous mix inside each pocket, followed by the spicy courgette slices and a drizzle of the yogurt mixture.

PER SERVING 470 kcals, protein 21g, carbs 48g, fat 21g, sat fat 4g, fibre 12g, sugar 8g, salt 1.9g

Bulghar & spinach fritters with eggs & tomato chutney

Bulghar wheat looks very similar to couscous, although it has a nuttier flavour and slightly larger grains. It is also far more nutritious than couscous.

TAKES 30 MINUTES ● SERVES 1

50g/2oz bulghar wheat
75g/2½oz spinach leaves
½ tsp ground cumin
½ shallot, finely chopped
½ garlic clove, chopped
handful fresh breadcrumbs
2 eggs, 1 beaten
1 tsp vegetable oil, plus extra
salad leaves, to serve

FOR THE CHUTNEY

1 tbsp sugar
1 tbsp white wine vinegar
½ shallot, finely chopped
85g/3oz cherry tomatoes, halved or
　　quartered

1 First make the chutney. In a pan, heat the sugar, vinegar and some salt. Add the shallot and tomatoes. Simmer for 1 minute, then remove from the heat.

2 Cook the bulghar wheat according to the pack instructions. Drain and tip into a bowl. Put the spinach in a colander and pour over boiling water. Cool with cold water, then squeeze out the excess water. Chop and add to the bulghar with the cumin, shallot, garlic and breadcrumbs. Blitz half in a food processor until it forms a chunky paste.

3 Return to the remaining half with a drizzle of the beaten egg and some seasoning. Mix together, adding a little more egg if needed. Shape into two patties and chill for at least 30 minutes.

4 Heat the oil in a non-stick frying pan, and fry the fritters until crisp. Fry the whole egg. Top the fritters with the fried egg, chutney, and salad leaves to serve.

PER SERVING 465 kcals, protein 18g, carbs 63g, fat 16g, sat fat 3g, fibre 4g, sugar 30g, salt 1g

Halloumi & aubergine burgers with harissa relish

Everyone loves a burger, and just because you're going meat free doesn't mean you have to miss out!

TAKES 20 MINUTES ● SERVES 1

2 tsp olive oil
1 shallot, finely sliced
½ small aubergine, cut into round slices
few slices halloumi
1 tsp soft brown sugar
1 small roasted red pepper from a jar, chopped
1 tsp harissa paste
1 ciabatta roll, halved and lightly toasted
1 tbsp houmous

1 Add a drizzle of the oil to a pan and tip in the shallot. Cook over a high heat for a few minutes, then turn down the heat and cook until soft and golden – about 8 minutes.

2 Meanwhile, heat another drizzle of the oil in a frying pan and fry the aubergine for a few minutes on each side until tender. Set aside. In the remaining oil, fry the halloumi until golden.

3 Tip the brown sugar, pepper and harissa into the onions. Cook for 1 minute until the sugar has melted. While the relish is cooking, spread the roll with houmous, laying halloumi and aubergine slices on top. Spoon the sticky, spicy relish over and serve.

PER SERVING 510 kcals, protein 22g, carbs 39g, fat 29g, sat fat 12g, fibre 5g, sugar 12g, salt 3.2g

Mushroom, walnut & tomato baked peppers

These healthy stuffed peppers are filled with tasty mushrooms and crunchy walnuts. You can swap the walnuts for almonds, pine nuts or hazelnuts, if you like.

TAKES 1 HOUR • SERVES 1

2 tsp sunflower oil
85g/3oz chestnut mushrooms, diced
1 small garlic clove, crushed
6 semi-dried tomato pieces in oil,
   drained well
25g/1oz dried white breadcrumbs
8–10 walnut halves, roughly chopped
small handful parsley, finely chopped
½ tsp dried chilli flakes
1 tbsp pesto
1 small red or yellow pepper
green salad, to serve

1 Heat oven to 220C/200C fan/gas 7. Heat the oil in a large frying pan and stir-fry the mushrooms over a high heat for 5 minutes. Season with a good grind of black pepper and remove from the heat. Stir in the garlic, tomato pieces, breadcrumbs, walnuts, chilli flakes, chopped parsley and pesto until thoroughly combined.

2 Cut the pepper in half from top to bottom. Carefully remove the seeds and membrane. Put in a small foil-lined roasting tin and fill each pepper half with the mushroom stuffing. Cover the surface of the stuffing with a small piece of foil. Bake for 35–40 minutes until tender. Serve with a green salad.

PER SERVING 621 kcals, protein 11g, carbs 30g, fat 51g, sat fat 7g, fibre 6g, sugar 10g, salt 2.4g

Wholewheat pasta with broccoli & almonds

This simple dish uses wholewheat pasta to give a nutty flavour and more texture. Add a few anchovies if you are not vegetarian and want a salty kick.

TAKES 20 MINUTES ● SERVES 1

1 tbsp extra-virgin olive oil
½ red chilli, deseeded and sliced (add extra chilli, if you like)
1 garlic clove, thinly sliced
100g/4oz wholewheat spaghetti
140g/5oz thin-stemmed broccoli, cut into pieces
zest ½ lemon
1 tbsp flaked toasted almonds
Parmesan shavings (or vegetarian alternative), to garnish

1 Bring a large pan of salted water to the boil. Meanwhile, heat the olive oil in a large frying pan. Add the chilli and garlic, and cook on a low heat until golden. Remove from the heat.

2 Add the pasta to the water and cook according to the pack instructions. In the final 4 minutes of cooking, add the broccoli. Once cooked, drain and tip into the garlic pan. Add the lemon zest and almonds, and toss together well. Serve in a bowl, topped with Parmesan or vegetarian-cheese shavings.

PER SERVING 638 kcals, protein 26g, carbs 82g, fat 23g, sat fat 3g, fibre 16g, sugar 6g, salt none

Coriander potato cakes with mango chutney

This thrifty dish makes a great speedy midweek meal – serve with salad and a big dollop of mango chutney.

TAKES 25 MINUTES • SERVES 1

140g/5oz floury potatoes, cut into chunks
1 medium egg, separated
small handful coriander leaves, chopped
2 spring onions, thinly sliced
zest ½ lemon
25g/1oz low-fat Cheddar, grated
½ red chilli, deseeded and chopped
25g/1oz dried breadcrumbs, toasted
1 tsp vegetable oil
dollop of mango chutney, to serve
green salad, to serve

1 Cook the potatoes in salted boiling water until tender. Drain and put back in the warm pan to dry out for a few minutes. Mash the potato, egg yolk, coriander and spring onions together. Season with sea salt and ground black pepper, and mix in the lemon zest, Cheddar and chilli. Shape into four or five small cakes.

2 Put the egg white in a bowl and whisk until foamy. Put the breadcrumbs on a plate. Dip the cakes in the egg white, allow the excess to drain off, then coat in the breadcrumbs, pressing to adhere well. Put on a baking sheet lined with baking parchment, cover and chill for 15 minutes or until ready to use.

3 Heat the vegetable oil in a large, heavy-based non-stick frying pan over a medium heat. Cook the cakes for 2–3 minutes each side, or until golden and heated through. Serve with a dollop chutney and some green salad.

PER SERVING 316 kcals, protein 17g, carbs 39g, fat 10g, sat fat 4g, fibre 3g, sugar 2g, salt 1.3g

Portobello & blue-cheese melts

You can swap the blue cheese for any other melty type of cheese– just make sure it's suitable for vegetarians if you are following a vegetarian diet.

TAKES 25 MINUTES • SERVES 1

1 red onion, cut into wedges
1 tsp olive oil
2 tbsp balsamic vinegar
2 Portobello or flat mushrooms
1 tsp thyme leaves
25g/1oz blue cheese
1 ciabatta roll
handful rocket leaves
oven fries and tomato ketchup, to
    serve (optional)

1 Heat oven to 220C/200C fan/gas 7. Mix the onion with the oil and vinegar, spread on a baking sheet, then put the mushrooms on top, stem-side up, and scatter over the thyme and some seasoning. Cook in the oven for 15 minutes, until starting to soften and caramelise.

2 Crumble the cheese into the cavity of the mushrooms and cook for 5 minutes more until the cheese is melted and bubbling.

3 Split the ciabatta roll in half and lightly toast. Top with a handful of rocket, the sticky onions and the cheese-topped mushrooms. Serve with oven fries, if you like.

PER SERVING 444 kcals, protein 20g, carbs 59g, fat 16g, sat fat 6g, fibre 6g, sugar 12g, salt 2.34g

Anytime eggs

Scrambled, poached or fried, eggs are a great staple supper. Make them the star of your plate in this one-pan fry-up.

TAKES 20 MINUTES • SERVES 1

1 tbsp olive oil
2–3 cooked potatoes, sliced
handful cherry tomatoes, sliced
2 spring onions, sliced
1 egg
few basil leaves, to garnish

1 Heat the oil in a frying pan, then add the potato slices and fry on both sides until brown. Add the tomatoes and spring onions, and fry for about 1 minute until softened.

2 Season with some salt and pepper, then make a space in the pan. Gently break the egg into the space and fry until cooked to your liking. Scatter over the basil leaves and serve.

PER SERVING 305 kcals, protein 11g, carbs 27g, fat 18g, sat fat 3g, fibre 2g, sugar 2g, salt 0.59g

Quinoa stew with squash, prunes & pomegranate

Get a dose of iron and protein from this healthy squash casserole that's full of texture and flavour.

TAKES 55 MINUTES • SERVES 1

140g/5oz butternut squash, cubed
2 tsp olive oil
1 shallot, thinly sliced
1 small garlic clove, chopped
1 tsp finely chopped ginger
½ tsp ras-el-hanout or Middle Eastern spice mix
50g/2oz quinoa
2 prunes, roughly chopped
juice ½ lemon
150ml/¼ pint vegetable stock
seeds from ½ pomegranate and small handful mint leaves, to garnish

1 Heat oven to 200C/180C fan/gas 6. Put the squash on a baking sheet and toss with half of the oil. Season well and roast for 30–35 minutes or until soft.
2 Meanwhile, heat the remaining oil in a big pan. Add the shallot, garlic and ginger, then season and cook for 10 minutes. Add the spice and quinoa, and cook for another couple of minutes. Add the prunes, lemon juice and stock, bring to the boil, then cover and simmer for 25 minutes.
3 When everything is tender, stir the squash through the quinoa stew. Spoon into a bowl and scatter with pomegranate seeds and mint to serve.

PER SERVING 318 kcals, protein 11g, carbs 50g, fat 9g, sat fat 1g, fibre 6g, sugar 20g, salt 0.5g

Tex-Mex burrito

This dish makes a hearty breakfast, lunch or supper. Add a few slices of crisp streaky bacon, if you want to add some meat.

TAKES 20 MINUTES ● SERVES 1

1 tomato, halved, seeds scooped out, then chopped
2 spring onions, chopped
½ red chilli, sliced (deseeded if you like it milder)
2 medium eggs
50ml/2fl oz milk
drizzle olive oil
50g/2oz Cheddar, grated
1 large wrap
soured cream and guacamole, to serve (optional)

1 In a small bowl, mix the tomato, half the spring onions and half the red chilli with some seasoning to make a salsa, and set aside. In another small bowl beat the eggs and milk with a fork with some seasoning.

2 Heat the oil in a large non-stick pan and fry the remaining spring onions and chilli for 1 minute, then pour in the egg mix. Gently scramble the eggs by dragging the egg mixture as it sets into the middle of the pan. Cook to your liking, then take off the heat and throw on the cheese. Stir through then put in the wrap.

3 Tuck up the top and bottom of the wrap and roll up, then slice in half and serve with the homemade tomato salsa and some soured cream and guacamole, if you like.

PER SERVING 611 kcals, protein 35g, carbs 33g, fat 38g, sat fat 16g, fibre 2g, sugar 6g, salt 1.96g

Harissa–aubergine kebabs with minty carrot salad

Harissa is a North African paste made from hot chilli peppers and spices. It's now available in most supermarkets. It varies in heat, so try a little bit before use.

TAKES 25 MINUTES • SERVES 1

1 tbsp harissa paste
1 tbsp red wine vinegar
½ aubergine, cut into 4cm/1½in cubes
1 carrot, finely shredded
½ small red onion, sliced
small handful mint, chopped, plus extra
　　leaves to garnish
1 Middle Eastern flatbread
1 heaped tbsp houmous
Greek yoghurt, to serve

1 Mix the harissa and vinegar in a bowl. Remove half and reserve. Toss the aubergine in the remaining harissa sauce and season. Thread on to metal or soaked wooden skewers. Heat a griddle or grill until hot, then cook the kebabs until golden on all sides and cooked through.

2 Meanwhile, mix together the carrot, onion and mint with some seasoning to make the salad.

3 Top the flatbread with the houmous, carrot salad and kebabs. Scatter over the extra mint and serve with yogurt and a drizzle of reserved harissa sauce.

PER SERVING 353 kcals, protein 13g, carbs 54g, fat 8g, sat fat 1g, fibre 13g, sugar 19g, salt 1.7g

Saucy Japanese greens with sticky sesame rice

We all need to eat more veggies, and this tasty recipe makes it so easy. Add some prawns if you're not following a vegetarian diet and want to bump up the protein.

TAKES 30 MINUTES ● SERVES 1

2 tsp caster sugar
75g/2½oz sushi rice
1 tsp sesame seeds, toasted
½ tsp sesame oil
1 tsp sunflower oil
140g/5oz long-stemmed broccoli
90g pack baby pak choi, each halved
    lengthways
3 spring onions, trimmed and halved
    lengthways

FOR THE SAUCE

1 tbsp brown miso paste
2 tsp mirin
2 tsp rice wine vinegar
1 tsp soft brown sugar
1 tsp finely grated ginger
½ red chilli, deseeded and diced

1 Stir together all the sauce ingredients with 2 teaspoons water. Set aside.

2 Bring a large pan of water to the boil with the caster sugar and a pinch of salt. Add the rice and boil for 15 minutes (or according to the pack instructions) until just cooked. Drain well and return to the pan. Sprinkle over the sesame seeds and sesame oil, then cover and set aside to keep warm.

3 Heat the sunflower oil in a wok until very hot, then toss in the broccoli and stir-fry for 2–3 minutes until almost tender, adding splashes of water occasionally to create steam. Add the pak choi and spring onions, and stir-fry for 30 seconds, then stir in the sauce and cook for a further 1–2 minutes, stirring constantly.

4 Serve the stir-fried veg on the rice, with the sauce poured over.

PER SERVING 552 kcals, protein 14g, carbs 91g, fat 14g, sat fat 2g, fibre 7g, sugar 32g, salt 2.1g

Spaghetti with caramelised onion, kale & blue cheese

If you've ever tried curly kale and thought you didn't like it, this is the recipe to change your mind.

TAKES 30 MINUTES • SERVES 1

2 tsp olive oil
1 small red onion, halved and sliced
1 tsp chopped thyme leaves
pinch dried chilli flakes
1 tbsp red wine vinegar
1 tsp caster sugar
50ml/2fl oz vegetable stock
100g/4oz spaghetti
50g/2oz curly kale, chopped
25g/1oz blue cheese, crumbled

1 Heat the oil in a frying pan. Add the onion, thyme and some seasoning. Sauté for 10 minutes until softened, then add the chilli flakes, vinegar, sugar and stock. Increase the heat and cook for another 5 minutes.

2 Meanwhile, boil a large pan of water, add some salt and cook the spaghetti according to the pack instructions, adding the kale for the final 4 minutes of cooking. Drain and return to the pot with a little of the cooking water. Tip in the onion mixture and half the cheese, and toss together. Serve topped with the remaining cheese.

PER SERVING 526 kcals, protein 21g, carbs 76g, fat 15g, sat fat 6g, fibre 10g, sugar 12g, salt 0.5g

Roasted squash with mozzarella & pesto

This sweet squash salad is the perfect garden supper – save it for a sunny day.

TAKES 55 MINUTES • SERVES 1

¼ butternut squash, sliced into
   2cm/¾in thick slices
2 tsp olive oil
pinch dried chilli flakes
½ small red onion, cut into thin wedges
½ red pepper, deseeded and cut into
   chunky pieces
handful rocket leaves
juice ½ lemon
50g/2oz mozzarella
1 tbsp fresh pesto

1 Heat oven to 220C/200C fan/gas 7. Put the squash on a large baking sheet. Toss with half the oil, the chilli and some seasoning. Bake for 15 minutes.

2 Take the sheet out of the oven and turn the squash. Scatter the onion and pepper over the top, and return to the oven for a further 25 minutes or until the vegetables are tender and lightly charred.

3 Toss the rocket leaves with the remaining oil, the lemon juice and some pepper. Pile on to a plate with the squash, onion and peppers on top. Tear the mozzarella over the salad and spoon over the pesto. Serve warm.

PER SERVING 277 kcals, protein 13g, carbs 26g, fat 14g, sat fat 3g, fibre 5g, sugar 16g, salt 0.4g

Katsu pork with sticky rice

Coat pork steaks in crisp Japanese breadcrumbs and serve with a sweet-and-spicy curry sauce. Look out for the speciality ingredients in large supermarkets.

TAKES 35 MINUTES ● SERVES 1

140g/5oz pork fillet or steak, trimmed
  of any fat
25g/1oz panko breadcrumbs
¼ tsp turmeric powder
1 tsp vegetable oil
1 egg white
coriander sprigs and pickled ginger,
  to garnish (optional)
cooked basmati or sushi rice, to serve

FOR THE SAUCE

1 tsp vegetable oil
½ small onion, chopped
1 small carrot, grated
½ eating apple, such as Braeburn,
  peeled, cored and roughly chopped
1 small garlic clove, sliced
½ tsp medium curry powder
pinch ground ginger
1 tsp tomato purée
½ tsp clear honey
1 tsp soy sauce
1 tsp cornflour
100ml/3½fl oz chicken stock
½ tsp sesame oil

1 For the sauce, heat the oil in a pan and add the onion, carrot and apple. Cover and cook gently, stirring, for 10 minutes until softened. Uncover, add the garlic, turn up the heat and cook for 1 minute.

2 Stir in the curry powder and ginger, then the tomato purée, honey, soy and cornflour. Stir in the stock and simmer for 5 minutes. Blitz until smooth, with a hand blender, then season with the sesame oil and some salt and pepper.

3 Put the pork between two sheets of cling film and bash with a rolling pin until the meat is 1cm/½in thick. In a shallow bowl, rub together the crumbs, turmeric and oil with some seasoning. Beat the egg white with a fork until a little frothy.

4 Heat oven to 220C/200C fan/gas 7. Dip the pork into the egg, then the crumbs, before transferring to a sheet. Bake the pork for 10–15 minutes. Serve with rice and the katsu sauce, garnished with coriander and pickled ginger, if you like.

PER SERVING 535 kcals, protein 37g, carbs 73g, fat 11g, sat fat 2g, fibre 4g, sugar 11g, salt 1.6g

Mustardy chop & chips

To cut down the cooking time, simply serve this mustardy pork chop and salad with oven chips.

TAKES 45 MINUTES ● SERVES 1

140g/5oz floury potatoes, cut into thin chips, patted dry
1 tbsp olive oil, plus a drizzle
pinch fennel seeds, crushed
pinch smoked paprika
100g/4oz green beans
½ tsp white wine vinegar
½ small shallot, finely chopped
pinch sugar
2 tsp Dijon mustard
1 pork chop
salad leaves, to serve (optional)

1 Heat oven to 220C/200C fan/gas 7. Toss the potatoes with 2 teaspoons of the oil and some seasoning on a baking sheet. Spread out in a single layer and bake for 20 minutes. Add the fennel seeds and paprika, turn the potatoes and bake for 20 minutes more until golden.

2 Meanwhile, cook the green beans in boiling water for 5–6 minutes. Run under cold water and drain well. Mix the remaining oil, the vinegar, shallot, sugar, 1 teaspoon of the mustard and some seasoning in a bowl. Toss the green beans in the dressing.

3 Rub a drizzle of the oil on the chop and season. Pan-fry for 7 minutes on each side until cooked through. Make sure to brown the fat on the edge, too. Smear with the remaining mustard and rest for a few minutes. Serve with the chips and bean salad and salad leaves, drizzling over the mustardy resting juices.

PER SERVING 691 kcals, protein 38g, carbs 33g, fat 45g, sat fat 15g, fibre 7g, sugar 5g, salt 0.7g

Sausage & fennel meatballs with lentils

If you love sausage and mash, this lighter alternative is sure to go down a treat.

TAKES 1 HOUR ● SERVES 1

2 good-quality sausages
¼ tsp fennel seeds, crushed
1 tsp olive oil
½ small onion, finely chopped
1 small carrot, finely chopped
¼ fennel bulb, trimmed and finely sliced
1 small garlic clove, crushed
50g/2oz Puy lentils
1 tsp tomato purée
225ml/8fl oz hot chicken or beef stock
squeeze lemon juice
handful parsley, chopped, to garnish

1 Squeeze the meat from the sausages into a large bowl. Add the fennel seeds and mix well with your hands. Shape the meat into walnut-sized balls.

2 Heat a drizzle of the oil in a large non-stick frying pan. Fry the meatballs for 5 minutes, turning regularly, until golden. Remove to a plate.

3 Add the rest of the oil to the pan, tip in the onion, carrots and fennel, cover and let the veg sweat over a gentle heat for 10 minutes until softened. Stir now and then.

4 Uncover the vegetables, turn up the heat until they start to colour. Stir in the garlic and let it sizzle for 1 minute. Stir in the lentils, tomato purée and stock. Cover and simmer for 25 minutes until the lentils are almost tender. Add the sausageballs. Cover and simmer for a further 10 minutes until the meat is cooked through. Squeeze over the lemon juice, season to taste and scatter with parsley to serve.

PER SERVING 533 kcals, protein 35g, carbs 42g, fat 25g, sat fat 8g, fibre 10g, sugar 11g, salt 2.8g

Lamb tagliata with watercress & tomatoes

The juicy pink lamb is the real star of this dish; buy a good-quality lamb steak from your butcher. Leaving it to come to room temperature will ensure it cooks perfectly.

TAKES 10 MINUTES, PLUS 30 MINUTES MARINATING • SERVES 1

few sprigs rosemary, needles chopped
2 tsp extra-virgin olive oil
140g/5oz piece boneless lamb leg steak or steak cut from lamb rump (get this from your butcher)
50g/2oz baby plum tomatoes
1 tsp redcurrant jelly
2 tsp balsamic vinegar
1 tsp capers, drained and rinsed
good handful watercress, thick stems removed
25g/1oz feta, crumbled
good crusty bread, to serve

1 Rub the rosemary and 1 teaspoon of the oil over the lamb. Leave to marinate for 30 minutes at room temperature.
2 Heat a frying pan until very hot. Wipe most of the rosemary from the lamb, then season the steak with plenty of salt and black pepper. Add the steak and the tomatoes to the pan. Sear the meat for 2 minutes on one side until golden, then turn and cook for 2 minutes more. This will give pink lamb. Transfer the meat and tomatoes to a plate and leave to rest.
3 Take the pan from the heat. Spoon in the redcurrant jelly, pour in the vinegar and remaining oil, then whisk to make a warm dressing. Add the capers, plus any juices from the lamb plate.
4 Slice the lamb thickly on an angle. Spread over a platter with the watercress and tomatoes, then finish with a crumbling of cheese. Spoon over the warm dressing and enjoy straight away with crusty bread.

PER SERVING 334 kcals, protein 28g, carbs 6g, fat 22g, sat fat 8g, fibre 2g, sugar 6g, salt 1.4g

Chicken livers & chorizo on toast

If you don't think you like livers, this could be the dish to change your mind. Give the chorizo enough time in the pan to leak its paprika-slicked oils before adding the livers.

TAKES 30 MINUTES ● SERVES 1

knob butter
½ shallot, finely chopped
1 garlic clove, ½ crushed, ½ left whole
85g/3oz cooking chorizo, skin removed, sliced
2 thick slices bread
1 tsp olive oil
140g/5oz chicken livers, trimmed of any sinew or tubes
good splash dry sherry (Fino works well)
2 tbsp single cream
small handful parsley, chopped

1 Melt the butter in a frying pan. When sizzling, add the shallot and the crushed garlic, and stir around the pan for 1–2 minutes to soften. Add the chorizo and cook for 4 minutes over a medium heat to release some of the oils.

2 Meanwhile, heat a griddle pan until hot. Drizzle the slices of bread with the olive oil and rub the remaining garlic all over the surface. Put on the griddle pan and cook for 1 minute each side until nicely charred with lines.

3 Turn up the heat under the chorizo pan, add the chicken livers and sear for 1 minute. Add the sherry, bubble for 1 minute more, add the cream and parsley, then season well. Put the bread on a plate and top with the chicken liver mixture.

PER SERVING 704 kcals, protein 49g, carbs 42g, fat 37g, sat fat 16g, fibre 3g, sugar 6g, salt 2.6g

Balsamic steak with peppercorn wedges

Treat yourself with this delicious variation on the classic steak and chips.

**TAKES 30 MINUTES, PLUS
MARINATING ● SERVES 1**

1 tbsp balsamic vinegar

1 tsp concentrated liquid beef stock or
1 jelly stock pot

½ garlic clove, finely grated

1 tsp wholegrain mustard

1 tsp clear honey

2 tsp olive oil

140g/5oz sirloin steak, about 5cm/2in
thick

mixed salad or peas, to serve (optional)

FOR THE WEDGES

1 large potato, such as King Edward,
cut into wedges

1 tbsp sunflower oil, plus extra for
greasing

1 tsp thyme leaves

1 tsp green peppercorns, crushed

1 Mix together the vinegar, stock, garlic, mustard, honey and olive oil in a large shallow bowl, then grind in some black pepper, but no salt. Add the steak and turn to coat. Leave to marinate in the fridge for 1 hour, or preferably overnight.

2 Heat oven to 220C/200C fan/gas 7. Toss the potatoes in a large bowl with the oil, thyme and peppercorns. Spread out on a greased baking sheet and bake for 30 minutes until the potatoes are crisp and golden.

3 Meanwhile cook the steak. Heat some oil in a frying pan. Wipe most of the marinade off the steak. When the pan is hot, add the steak and cook to your liking. Serve with the wedges and some mixed salad or peas, if you like.

PER SERVING 534 kcals, protein 34g, carbs 43g, fat 25g, sat fat 8g, fibre 5g, sugar 4g, salt 0.3g

Sushi rice bowl with beef, egg & chilli sauce

The fried egg on top of this dish acts as a silky sauce to coat the rice, veggies and beef, so make sure you don't overcook the yolk.

TAKES 30 MINUTES ● SERVES 1

75g/2½oz sushi rice

140g/5oz rump steak, thinly sliced

1 small garlic clove, chopped

2 tsp soy sauce

pinch sugar

1 tbsp sesame oil

1 medium egg

1 small carrot, cut into long matchsticks

½ small courgette, cut into long matchsticks

1 tbsp chilli sauce

1 Boil the sushi rice in a large pan with a lid in plenty of water – it should take about 8–10 minutes – until it is just cooked and still has a bite to it. Drain, put back in the pan, cover with a lid and set aside.

2 Mix the steak with the garlic, soy sauce, sugar and a grind of black pepper. You will need two frying pans or one frying pan and a wok: divide the oil between the two pans and heat until just smoking. Fry the egg to your liking, then set aside. In the other pan, brown the beef for 1–2 minutes, then remove and keep warm. Tip the vegetables into the pan, stir-fry for 1 minute, then push to one side; add the rice and cook for 1 minute more to heat through.

3 Put the rice, veg and beef in a bowl. Slide the egg on top and drizzle with the chilli sauce.

PER SERVING 621 kcals, protein 41g, carbs 63g, fat 23g, sat fat 5g, fibre 2g, sugar 8g, salt 3.2g

Braised beef with anchovy toasts

This is a real winter warmer. Don't be put off by the anchovies– they add a delicious salty, savoury depth of flavour to the stew and crispy toasts.

TAKES 2½ HOURS • SERVES 1

2 tsp olive oil

3 shallots, 1 finely chopped, others peeled and left whole

1 small garlic clove, finely chopped

1 bay leaf

85ml/3fl oz red wine

125ml/4fl oz beef stock

½ tsp caster sugar

½ tsp plain flour

2 tsp tomato purée

140g/5oz lean beef skirt, cut into large chunks

1 anchovy in oil, chopped

4–5 Chantenay carrots, stalk ends trimmed, or 1 carrot chopped into chunks

5 Kalamata olives

FOR THE ANCHOVY TOASTS

1 anchovy in oil

knob unsalted butter

2 tsp finely chopped parsley, plus extra to garnish

2 slices French stick

1 Heat the oil in a large heavy-based casserole dish and fry the chopped shallot for 5 minutes. Stir in the garlic and bay leaf, and fry for 2 minutes more.

2 Pour in the wine, stock and sugar. Mix the flour with the tomato purée and 1 tablespoon water. Tip the flour paste into the wine mixture and stir continuously until thickened. Then add the meat and anchovy, cover and leave to simmer on the hob for 1 hour.

3 Stir in the whole shallots, carrots and olives. Cover and simmer for 1 hour more until everything is tender. Meanwhile, for the anchovy toasts, grind the anchovy fillet using a pestle and mortar until smooth (or very finely chop), then beat into the butter with the parsley and lots of black pepper.

4 To serve, grill the slices of French stick until lightly toasted, then spread with the anchovy butter. Serve on top of the beef stew and scatter with parsley.

PER SERVING 740 kcals, protein 65g, carbs 29g, fat 37g, sat fat 15g, fibre 5g, sugar 14g, salt 3.04g

Lamb & apricot stew

This North African-inspired stew is sweet and spicy, perfect served with fluffy couscous. Leave it to simmer on a really low heat for up to 2 hours for tender lamb.

TAKES 55 MINUTES • SERVES 1

1 tbsp olive oil
140g/5oz stewing lamb pieces
1 shallot, thinly sliced
1 small garlic clove, chopped
2 tsp chopped ginger
1 tsp ras-el-hanout, Berber or other
    Middle Eastern spice mix
2 tsp tomato purée
3 soft dried apricots, halved
150ml/¼ pint vegetable or chicken
    stock
mint or coriander leaves, to garnish
lemon wedges, to squeeze over
cooked couscous, to serve

1 In a medium-sized pan, heat half of the oil. Season the meat and fry briefly until browned. Remove the meat to a plate with a slotted spoon and add the remaining oil to the pan. Add the shallot, garlic and ginger, and fry with a little seasoning. Cook for 5 minutes until soft, then add the spice mix, tomato purée, apricots and stock, and return the lamb to the pan. Simmer gently for 45 minutes.

2 Serve sprinkled with, mint or coriander leaves, with lemon wedges for squeezing over and some fluffy couscous.

PER SERVING 447 kcals, protein 32g, carbs 19g, fat 28g, sat fat 10g, fibre 4g, sugar 15g, salt 0.69g

Warm lentil salad with Serrano, chicken & rocket

If you can't find ready-cooked Puy lentils, cook 50g/2oz dried lentils in plenty of water until tender. Don't add salt until they are cooked, or they will be tough.

TAKES 15 MINUTES ● SERVES 1

½ small red onion, very thinly sliced
1 tsp sherry vinegar, plus extra to drizzle (optional)
small handful flat-leaf parsley, roughly chopped
2–3 ripe tomatoes, roughly chopped
½ tsp small capers, drained
75g/2½oz ready-cooked Puy lentils
2 tsp extra-virgin olive oil
2 slices Serrano ham, torn into pieces
1 cooked chicken breast, torn into pieces
handful wild rocket leaves, to garnish

1 Put the onion in a bowl, drizzle over the vinegar, then season with salt and pepper. Set aside for 10 minutes or so until the onion has softened slightly.
2 Meanwhile, in another large bowl, mix the parsley and tomato with the capers. When ready to serve, tip the lentils into a sieve and rinse with boiling water from the kettle. Drain. Toss the onions and their juices into the lentils, then add half the olive oil and carefully mix everything together. Scoop this on to a plate, then top with the ham, chicken and rocket. Drizzle over the remaining olive oil and a little more vinegar, if you like, then serve.

PER SERVING 377 kcals, protein 36g, carbs 22g, fat 16g, sat fat 3g, fibre 7g, sugar 5g, salt 2.9g

Sticky lamb cutlets with warm bean & couscous salad

Look out for fig jam or conserve in the supermarket. If you can't find it, you can substitute redcurrant jelly.

TAKES 20 MINUTES ● **SERVES 1**

50g/2oz couscous
1 tbsp olive oil
3 lamb cutlets
85g/3oz green beans, ends trimmed
2 tbsp fig jam or conserve, mixed with
   1–2 tbsp water
1 tbsp balsamic vinegar
½ small red onion, thinly sliced
5 cherry tomatoes, halved
zest and juice ½ lemon
few mint leaves, most chopped, a few
   left whole to garnish

1 Heat a frying pan and bring a small pan of water to the boil. Put the couscous in a bowl, pour over 100ml/3fl oz boiling water from the kettle, cover with a tea towel and set aside. Rub a little of the oil and some seasoning on to each lamb cutlet. Cook the green beans in the boiling water for 4 minutes, then drain.
2 In the hot frying pan, cook the lamb for 3 minutes each side, brushing with the fig jam. Add the vinegar in the final minute of cooking, transfer the lamb to a plate and leave to rest. Bubble any remaining juices in the pan until sticky.
3 Mix the couscous with a fork to fluff it up, add the beans, red onion, tomatoes, lemon zest and juice, the chopped mint and the remaining oil. Mix and season. Spoon the salad on to your plate and top with the lamb cutlets. Drizzle over the remaining sticky juices from the pan and scatter over a few whole mint leaves.

PER SERVING 631 kcals, protein 39g, carbs 55g, fat 28g, sat fat 9g, fibre 4g, sugar 29g, salt 0.3g

Fish with chilli, mango & lime salsa

Cooking fish on the bone improves its flavour and helps to keep it moist. Served simply with a zingy salsa, it will remind you of tropical holidays in the sun.

TAKES 40 MINUTES ● SERVES 1

1 small whole fish (we used sea bream, but sea bass or mackerel would also work well), descaled and cleaned (ask your fishmonger to do this)
2 tsp Cajun seasoning
zest and juice ½ lime, plus extra ½ to squeeze over
1 tsp oil
100g tub ripe mango, chopped
½ red chilli, deseeded and finely chopped
½ small ripe avocado, peeled, stoned and diced
2 spring onions, sliced
small handful coriander leaves, chopped
100g/4oz green beans
boiled rice, to serve

1 Heat oven to 200C/180C fan/gas 6. Make three or four slashes on each side of the fish. Rub in the seasoning, lime zest and oil, making sure you get it right into the slashes and the cavity. Put on a baking sheet lined with foil and bake for 12–15 minutes or until just cooked through.

2 Heat grill to high and cook the fish for 2–3 minutes more under the grill to char the skin. Remove from the oven, cover and rest for a few minutes.

3 For the salsa, mix the mango, chilli, avocado, spring onions, coriander and lime juice, and season. Bring a small pan of water to the boil, add the beans and cook for 4 minutes, then drain. Serve the fish with some boiled rice, and the beans and salsa, and a lime half to squeeze over.

PER SERVING 552 kcals, protein 33g, carbs 29g, fat 34g, sat fat 7g, fibre 6g, sugar 6g, salt 0.5g

Mini masala chicken pie

Chicken tikka is a national favourite, but give it a new spin in this potato-topped pie.

TAKES 1 HOUR • SERVES 1

1 tsp vegetable oil
1 boneless skinless chicken breast, chopped into chunks
1 shallot, chopped
1 tsp grated ginger
1 small garlic clove, crushed
1 tsp medium curry powder
½ tsp ground coriander
½ tsp ground cumin
½ tsp black or brown mustard seeds
200g can chopped tomatoes
100ml/3½fl oz light coconut milk
1 small pepper, use any colour you like, deseeded and cut into large chunks
few sprigs coriander, leaves roughly chopped, stalks reserved and finely chopped

FOR THE TOPPING

2 floury potatoes (about 250g/9oz total), cut into large chunks
100ml/3½fl oz light coconut milk
¼ tsp turmeric powder
squeeze lemon juice
2 spring onions, finely chopped
¼ tsp nigella seeds

1 Heat a frying pan and add half the oil. Add the chicken and brown, then remove to a plate. Turn down the heat and add the remaining oil, the shallot, ginger and garlic. Fry until soft. Add the spices and cook for a few minutes, stirring.

2 Stir in the tomatoes and coconut milk. Bubble for 5 minutes. Return the chicken to the pan with the pepper. Simmer for 15 minutes until the sauce reduces. Take off the heat, stir in the coriander leaves.

3 For the topping, put the potatoes in a pan of water, bring to the boil, then cook for 10–15 minutes. Drain, then tip back into the pan and steam-dry for 3 minutes.

4 Add the coconut milk and turmeric to the pan, and mash. Season with the lemon juice and some salt, then stir in the spring onions and coriander stalks.

5 Heat oven to 200C/180C fan/gas 6. Put the chicken into an individual pie dish, dollop on the mash, then sprinkle over the nigella seeds. Bake for 25–30 minutes until hot through and crisping.

PER SERVING 570 kcals, protein 41g, carbs 57g, fat 21g, sat fat 13g, fibre 10g, sugar 15g, salt 0.5g

Cabbage & bean sauté with white fish

Any type of fish would work well in this recipe – why not try mackerel, sea bream or red mullet?

TAKES 45 MINUTES ● SERVES 1

small knob butter
1 rasher smoked streaky bacon, chopped
1 shallot, finely chopped
1 small celery stick, diced
1 small carrot, diced
few sprigs thyme
¼ Savoy cabbage, shredded
100ml/3½fl oz chicken stock
200g can white beans in water drained and rinsed, (we used flageolet)

FOR THE FISH

140g/5oz sustainable white fish fillet, skin on
1 tsp plain flour
2 tsp olive oil

1 Heat the butter in a large pan with a lid until starting to sizzle, add the bacon, then fry for a few minutes. Add the shallot, celery and carrot, then gently cook for 8–10 minutes until softening, but not brown. Stir in the thyme and cabbage, then cook for a few minutes until the cabbage starts to wilt. Add the stock and beans. Season, cover the pan, then simmer gently for 10 minutes until the cabbage is soft but still vibrant.

2 Meanwhile, cook the fish. Season the fillet, then dust the skin with flour. Heat the oil in a frying pan. Fry the fish, skin-side down, for 4 minutes until crisp, then flip over and finish on the flesh side until cooked through. Serve the fish fillet on top of a pile of cabbage

---

PER SERVING 423 kcals, protein 42g, carbs 29g, fat 16g, sat fat 4g, fibre none, sugar 13g, salt 1.45g

Smart crab linguine

Picking crab is a fiddly and time-consuming process. If you have the time, you can use fresh but, if not, a pot of ready picked crab meat from the fishmonger is just as good.

TAKES 15 MINUTES ● SERVES 1

100g/4oz linguine
1 tbsp olive oil
2 garlic cloves, finely sliced
2 tbsp low-fat crème fraîche
100g tub white crabmeat or 100g
   drained from a can
handful rocket leaves, chopped, plus
   extra leaves to garnish
zest ½ lemon
1 tbsp toasted pine nuts

1 Cook the linguine according to the pack instructions, reserving a little cooking liquid before you drain it.
2 Meanwhile, heat the olive oil in a frying pan. Add the garlic and cook gently to soften, but don't brown. Stir in the crème fraîche, crabmeat, chopped rocket and lemon zest, and gently heat through.
3 Tip in the cooked pasta and a little cooking liquid to help the sauce coat the pasta. Season and give everything a stir. Sprinkle with the pine nuts and extra rocket leaves.

PER SERVING 753 kcals, protein 35g, carbs 76g, fat 34g, sat fat 7g, fibre 4g, sugar 4g, salt 1.1g

Sizzled masala lamb with chopped salad

If you have time, leave the lamb chops to marinade for up to 24 hours before cooking as this will really enhance the flavour.

TAKES 20 MINUTES, PLUS MARINATING (OPTIONAL) ● SERVES 1

1 tsp rapeseed oil

1 tbsp curry paste, we used tikka masala

2 lamb loin chops

seeds from ½ pomegranate

¼ cucumber, peeled, deseeded and finely diced

6 radishes, diced

6 cherry tomatoes, quartered

½ small red onion, very finely sliced

small handful each mint and coriander leaves, roughly chopped, plus a few whole leaves to garnish

¼ tsp ground cumin

juice ½ lemon

1 Heat grill to high. Rub the oil and curry paste all over the chops and season. Put the chops on a baking sheet and grill for about 4–5 minutes each side for medium, depending on the thickness of the chop, or to your liking. Allow to rest for a couple of minutes.

2 Meanwhile, put the remaining ingredients (except the garnish) in a bowl, give everything a stir, then season. Spoon the salad on to a plate and lay the chops on top. Scatter with the remaining herb leaves.

PER SERVING 568 kcals, protein 39g, carbs 20g, fat 36g, sat fat 14g, fibre 6g, sugar 17g, salt 0.9g

Smoked haddock with lemon & dill lentils

This healthy supper is packed with nutrients and is especially high in protein, meaning you'll stay fuller for longer.

TAKES 30 MINUTES ● SERVES 1

50g/2oz Puy lentils
1 small shallot, finely chopped
1 small carrot, finely chopped
1 small celery stick, finely chopped
150ml/¼ pint vegetable stock
1 tbsp half-fat crème fraîche
1 tbsp chopped dill leaves
zest ½ lemon
100g/4oz smoked haddock fillet
handful baby leaf spinach

1 Tip the lentils into a pan with the shallot, carrot and celery. Pour in the stock and bring to the boil. Give it all a stir, then reduce the heat, cover and simmer for 20–25 minutes, until the lentils are tender.

2 In a small bowl, mix together the crème fraîche, half the dill and the lemon zest, adding a little seasoning. Put the fish in a shallow dish with a splash of water and cover with cling film. Microwave on Medium for 4–6 minutes until the fish flakes easily.

3 When the lentils are cooked, stir in the spinach until the leaves are barely wilted, then stir in the crème-fraîche mixture. Spoon the lentil mix on to a warmed plate and top with the haddock. Scatter over the remaining dill and serve.

PER SERVING 288 kcals, protein 33g, carbs 30g, fat 4g, sat fat 1g, fibre 7g, sugar 7g, salt 2.5g

One-pan duck with Savoy cabbage

Who says duck is just for special occasions? This one-pan dinner is quick and easy, and still feels like a real treat.

TAKES 30 MINUTES ● **SERVES 1**

1 duck breast
140g/5oz cooked new potatoes, thickly sliced
few sprigs flat-leaf parsley, roughly chopped
½ small garlic clove, finely chopped
1 rasher smoked streaky bacon, chopped
¼ small Savoy cabbage, trimmed, quartered, cored and finely sliced
1 tsp balsamic vinegar
½ tsp olive oil

1 Lightly score the skin of the duck breast, then season with some salt and pepper. Lay the duck breast, skin-side down, in a non-stick pan, then put over a low heat. Leave for 15 minutes to brown, then flip on to the flesh side for 5 minutes.

2 Remove the duck from the pan (keep warm on a foil-covered plate) then turn up the heat. Add the potatoes to the pan, fry until brown and crisp, then scatter over the parsley and garlic. Scoop out with a slotted spoon on to the duck plate, then season with salt and keep warm.

3 Keep the pan on the heat. Fry the bacon until crisp, then add the cabbage. Cook for 1 minute, add a splash of water, then fry for 2 minutes, until the cabbage is wilted. Whisk the vinegar and olive oil.

4 To serve, carve the duck breast into slices. Fan out on a plate, spoon cabbage on one side and the potatoes on the other. Drizzle over the dressing.

PER SERVING 611 kcals, protein 29g, carbs 28g, fat 43g, sat fat 13g, fibre 8g, sugar 9g, salt 1.1g

Griddled bananas with nutty chocolate custard

Melt dark chocolate into a pot of low-fat custard for a quick and tasty dessert.

TAKES 5 MINUTES • SERVES 1

1 small ripe banana, peeled and sliced
    at an angle into 2cm/½in slices
150g pot low-fat custard
2 squares dark chocolate
2 tsp chopped toasted hazelnuts

1 Heat a griddle pan to a high heat. Cook the banana slices for 2–3 minutes each side until charred.

2 Meanwhile, remove the lid from the custard and push in the chocolate. Microwave on High for 1 minute. Remove and leave to stand for 1 minute, then stir well. Tip the custard into a bowl, add the hot bananas and sprinkle with hazelnuts.

PER SERVING 349 kcals, protein 8g, carbs 55g, fat 11g, sat fat 4g, fibre 2g, sugar 46g, salt 0.4g

Banoffee split

A retro classic gets a makeover with an indulgent hot Mars bar sauce.

TAKES 5 MINUTES ● SERVES 1

1 small ripe banana
2 scoops ice cream

FOR THE SAUCE

1 fun size Mars bar, chopped into small
  chunks
3 tbsp single cream
small knob butter

1 Tip all the sauce ingredients into a small saucepan and heat gently, stirring until you have a smooth sauce.
2 Peel and split the banana. Put onto a plate, add the scoops of ice cream, drizzle over the warm sauce and serve straight away.

PER SERVING 50502 kcals, protein 8g, carbs 54g, fat 28g, sat fat 17g, fibre 1g, sugar 50g, salt 0.4g

Yogurt parfait with crushed strawberries & amaretti

A healthy treat for when you want something sweet without packing in the calories.

TAKES 10 MINUTES • SERVES 1

85g/3oz strawberries, chopped
2 tsp caster sugar
100g pot low-fat Greek yogurt
2 small amaretti biscuits, crushed

1 In a small bowl, mix the strawberries with half the sugar, then roughly mash the berries with a fork so they are juicy. Mix the remaining sugar into the yogurt, then layer up in a glass with amaretti biscuits, the sweetened yogurt and crushed strawberries.

PER SERVING 182 kcals, protein 6g, carbs 29g, fat 5g, sat fat 3g, fibre 1g, sugar 22g, salt 0.31g

Drop scones with strawberry compote

Whip up a quick batch of drop scones for dessert tonight– they'll be on the table in 10 minutes flat!

TAKES 10 MINUTES ● SERVES 1

FOR THE COMPOTE

100g/4oz ripe strawberries, hulled then halved or quartered

1 tbsp caster sugar

2 tsp lemon juice

few drops balsamic vinegar (optional)

FOR THE DROP SCONES

50g/2oz self-raising flour

1 tsp white caster sugar, plus extra for tossing

1 medium egg

¼ tsp vanilla extract

2–4 tbsp semi-skimmed milk

knob butter

vanilla ice cream, to serve

1 Put the strawberries in a lidded pan with the sugar and lemon juice. Heat gently until the sugar dissolves, then bring to a simmer. Cover the pan and simmer for 3 minutes, until syrupy, then cool. Add the balsamic vinegar, if using.

2 Now make the drop scones. Mix the flour and sugar in a bowl. Make a well in the middle, crack in the egg. Add the vanilla and a splash of the milk. Whisk until thick and smooth. Add more milk if it needs loosening.

3 Heat a non-stick frying pan, then add the butter. Spoon in dessert spoons of the batter, spacing them well apart, to make drop scones about 7.5cm/3in wide. As soon as bubbles appear on the surface, flip the scones and cook until puffed in the middle. Toss the scones in the extra caster sugar, then serve with the strawberry compote and a scoop of ice cream.

PER SERVING 332 kcals, protein 7g, carbs 60g, fat 8g, sat fat 4g, fibre 3g, sugar 35g, salt 0.7g

Blackberry & lemon mess

Eton mess is a classic British dessert, and one of the easiest to make. Swap the blackberries for any soft fruit you can get your hands on, but berries work the best.

TAKES 10 MINUTES ● SERVES 1
150ml/¼ pint whipping cream
2 tsp icing sugar
1 tbsp lemon curd
2 ready-made meringue nests
50g/2oz blackberries

1 Tip the cream into a bowl, sift in the icing sugar and gently whip until soft peaks just hold a little shape.

2 Dollop the lemon curd over the whipped cream, then crumble over the meringues in small chunks. Put the blackberries into another bowl and lightly rough up with a fork so they're still whole but juicy, then scatter them over the lemony meringue cream.

3 Fold together with a large spatula or spoon, just a few times to marble everything through. Spoon into a glass or bowl, and eat straight away.

PER SERVING 560 kcals, protein 3g, carbs 44g, fat 41g, sat fat 26g, fibre 1g, sugar 41g, salt 0.1g

Choc-chip, banana & peanut-butter pancakes

Whip up a couple of lacy thin pancakes or buy some French crêpes from the supermarket, then fill with this indulgent combination.

TAKES 10 MINUTES ● SERVES 1

2 pancakes
1 tbsp smooth peanut butter
2 tsp icing sugar
splash milk
1 tbsp chocolate chips
½ sliced banana
a few chopped peanuts, to sprinkle
    (optional)

1 Prepare or warm your pancakes. Mix the peanut butter with the icing sugar, milk and chocolate chips. Spread the choc-chip mix over the pancakes. Top with the banana slices. Fold up and sprinkle with a few chopped peanuts, if you like.

PER SERVING 621 kcals, protein 14g, carbs 64g, fat 34g, sat fat 13g, fibre 3g, sugar 44g, salt 0.4g

Lemon French toast with poached plums

A great recipe for using up leftovers– you can use white bread, brioche or even croissants. Bread that is a few days' old works the best.

TAKES 20 MINUTES • **SERVES 1**

1 medium egg, beaten
4 tbsp milk
zest ½ lemon
1 tbsp caster sugar, plus extra to
  sprinkle (optional)
1 slice bread or brioche, cut in half
  diagonally
knob butter
4 small plums or 2 large ones, halved
  and stoned
squeeze lemon juice
crème fraîche or vanilla ice cream,
  to serve (optional)

1 Mix the egg, milk, lemon zest and half the sugar in a shallow dish. Add the bread, then turn in the liquid until well soaked.

2 Put the remaining sugar and a little of the butter in a frying pan, then heat gently until the sugar has melted. Add the plums, then fry until they are softened and the juice is golden brown, about 5 minutes. Add the lemon juice, then heat gently to make a light syrup.

3 Heat a little more of the butter in a large non-stick frying pan, then add the slices of bread and fry on each side until golden brown. Put on to a plate, sprinkle with a little extra sugar, if you like, then spoon over the plums and their juices. Serve as it is or with a dollop of crème fraîche or scoop of vanilla ice cream.

PER SERVING (without crème fraîche or ice cream) 331 kcals, protein 8g, carbs 44g, fat 15g, sat fat 8g, fibre 2g, sugar 28g, salt 0.78g

Quick plum crumble

This superspeedy pud is even better served with lashings of cream or hot custard.

TAKES 20 MINUTES • SERVES 1

3–4 plums, stoned and quartered
1 tbsp sugar
50g/2oz Madeira cake, diced into cubes
2 tbsp double cream, plus extra to
   serve (optional)
small handful flaked almonds or
   chopped pistachios
icing sugar, for dusting
hot custard, to serve (optional)

1 Heat oven to 180C/160C fan/gas 4. Simmer the plums in a pan over a low heat with 2 tablespoons water and the sugar until softened. Tip into a small baking dish and scatter over the Madeira cake.

2 Drizzle with double cream, scatter with the nuts and dust with icing sugar. Bake for 10–15 minutes, just until browning. Serve with extra cream or hot custard, if you like.

PER SERVING 327 kcals, protein 4g, carbs 46g, fat 14g, sat fat 7g, fibre 4g, sugar 40g, salt 0.4g

Peach & almond slice

You can freeze any leftover pastry from this recipe in 100g/4oz portions for 2 months; simply defrost overnight in the fridge every time to make this simple dessert.

TAKES 25 MINUTES • SERVES 1

100g/4oz piece puff pastry
1 egg yolk, beaten
50g/2oz marzipan, chopped
1 small peach, halved, stoned and
thinly sliced
1 tsp flaked almonds
crème fraîche, to serve

1 Heat oven to 220C/200C fan/gas 7. Roll out the pastry until roughly 10cm/4in in diameter, trim to a square. Lay the pastry sheet on a baking sheet. Use a knife to mark a 1cm/½in border – be careful not to go all the way through. Prick inside the border with a fork, then brush all over with beaten egg yolk.
2 Bake for 10 minutes until golden and slightly risen. Top with the marzipan and fan out the peach slices on top, followed by a sprinkling of almonds.
3 Put the slice back into the oven for 10 minutes until puffed up and golden. Serve with a dollop of crème fraîche.

PER SERVING 408 kcals, protein 7g, carbs 42g, fat 25g, sat fat 8g, fibre 2g, sugar 25g, salt 0.69g

Iced-coffee sundae

This ice-cream-smoothie sundae is a coffee lover's dream on a hot summer's day.
Keep a tub of ice cream in the freezer for a quick pud any time you need it!

TAKES 5 MINUTES ● SERVES 1

1 shot cold espresso coffee or
   25ml/1fl oz strong black coffee
200ml/7fl oz full-fat milk
3 scoops vanilla ice cream
2 ice cubes
1 small brownie or chocolate chip
   cookie

1 Pour the espresso or strong coffee and the milk into a blender. Add 2 scoops of the ice cream and the ice cubes, then blitz until it is the consistency of a smoothie. Pour straight into a tall glass, top with the last scoop of ice cream and crumble over the brownie or cookie to finish.

PER SERVING 575 kcals, protein 14g, carbs 66g, fat 30g, sat fat 19g, fibre 1g, sugar 36g, salt 0.7g

Spiced hot choc

*This cinnamon-spiked hot chocolate is just the thing when you fancy something sweet
– better yet, it's low in fat. Dunk in a few biscuits if you're not counting the calories!*

TAKES 5 MINUTES • SERVES 1
250ml skimmed milk
1–2 squares dark chocolate
pinch ground cinnamon
dribble clear honey
biscuits, to serve (optional)

1 Fill a mug with skimmed milk. Add the
dark chocolate, cinnamon and honey,
and heat in the microwave until hot.
Serve with biscuits for dipping, if you like.

PER SERVING 181 kcals, protein 10g, carbs 18g,
fat 7g, sat fat 4g, fibre 2g, sugar 17g, salt 0.3g

Index

Also available from BBC Books and *Good Food*

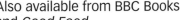